Contents

Spicy Sausage Pizza with Peperonata & Red Onion

MAKES 2 (12- TO 14-INCH) PIZZAS OR 4 PERSONAL PIZZAS

PREP TIME: 15 minutes
COOK TIME: 25 minutes
TOTAL TIME: 50 minutes

Ingredients:

Cornmeal or flour, for dusting
- 1 tablespoon extra-virgin olive oil, plus more for brushing
- 2 hot Italian sausage links (about ½ pound), casings removed
- Simply Amazing Pizza Dough
- ¾ cup White Sauce
- 2 garlic cloves, minced
- ¾ cup grated mozzarella cheese
- 3 tablespoons grated Parmesan cheese
- ¼ cup Peperonata
- 1 small red onion, sliced thin
- 2 fresh oregano sprigs, stemmed and chopped
- ½ teaspoon fine sea salt
- ¼ teaspoon freshly ground black pepper

Direction:

1. Preheat the oven and pizza stone (if using) to 500°F. Dust a pizza peel with cornmeal (if using a pizza stone), or brush two baking sheets with olive oil.

2. In a sauté pan over medium-high heat, heat the olive oil. Add the sausage and cook, breaking it up with a wooden spoon, until no longer pink, 4 to 6 minutes. Use a slotted spoon to transfer the cooked sausage to a medium bowl.

3. Roll out one of the dough balls to the desired size, and place it on the pizza peel (if using a pizza stone) or on the prepared baking sheet.

4. Leaving a 1-inch border, spoon half of the White Sauce evenly onto the dough. Sprinkle with half of the minced garlic, then top with half of the mozzarella and grated Parmesan. Finish with half of the Peperonata and red onion slices.

5. Transfer the pizza to the hot pizza stone or oven rack, and bake until the crust is golden and the cheese has melted, 5 to 7 minutes on the pizza stone or 7 to 10 minutes on the baking sheet.

6. Remove the pizza from the oven and transfer it to a cutting board. Let it rest for 5 minutes, then sprinkle with half of the oregano, salt, and pepper. Slice and serve.

7. Repeat from step 3 with the remaining dough ball and toppings.

Chorizo Pizza with Prosciutto, Olives & Piquillo Peppers

MAKES 2 (12- TO 14-INCH) PIZZAS OR 4 PERSONAL PIZZAS

PREP TIME: 15 minutes
COOK TIME: 30 minutes
TOTAL TIME: 50 minutes

Ingredients:

- Cornmeal or flour, for dusting
- 2 tablespoons extra-virgin olive oil, plus extra for brushing
- 3 fresh chorizo sausage links
- Simply Amazing Pizza Dough
- 1 cup New York–Style Pizza Sauce
- 1 cup grated mozzarella cheese
- 4 smoked piquillo peppers, drained and sliced lengthwise
- 4 slices prosciutto, torn into small pieces
- ¼ cup halved black olives
- ¼ cup chopped fresh flat-leaf parsley
- ½ cup grated manchego cheese
- ⅛ teaspoon freshly ground black pepper

Direction:

1. Preheat the oven and pizza stone (if using) to 500°F. Dust a pizza peel with cornmeal (if using a pizza stone), or brush two baking sheets with olive oil.

2. In a medium skillet over medium heat, heat the oil until hot but not smoking. Add the sausages and cook for 7 to 10 minutes, turning occasionally, until they are browned on all sides. Remove the skillet from the heat and set it aside to cool. When the chorizo is cool enough to handle, cut it into thin slices.

3. Roll out one of the dough balls to the desired size, and place it on the pizza peel (if using a pizza stone) or on the prepared baking sheet.

4. Leaving a 1-inch border, spoon the sauce evenly onto the pizza. Top with half of the mozzarella cheese, followed by half of the piquillo peppers. Scatter half of the chorizo and prosciutto over the pizza, followed by half of the olives and parsley.

5. Transfer the pizza to the hot pizza stone or oven rack, and bake until the crust is golden and the cheese has melted, 5 to 7 minutes on the pizza stone or 7 to 10 minutes on the baking sheet.

6. Remove the pizza from the oven, transfer it to a cutting board, and let it rest for 5 minutes. Top with half of the manchego and pepper, slice, and serve.

7. Repeat from step 3 with the remaining dough ball and toppings.

Prosciutto Cotto Pizza with Pesto & Spring Garlic

MAKES 2 (12- TO 14-INCH) PIZZAS OR 4 PERSONAL PIZZAS

PREP TIME: 10 minutes
COOK TIME: 20 minutes
TOTAL TIME: 35 minutes
Ingredients:

- Cornmeal or flour, for dusting, or extra-virgin olive oil, for brushing
- Simply Amazing Pizza Dough
- 4 stalks spring garlic or ramps, white and light green parts finely chopped, or 2 garlic cloves, sliced thin
- ¾ cup Basil Pesto
- ½ pound fresh mozzarella cheese, shredded or cut into small pieces
- ¾ cup fresh ricotta cheese
- ¼ pound prosciutto cotto or Virginia ham, chopped into bite-size pieces
- ⅛ teaspoon salt
- ⅛ teaspoon freshly ground black pepper

Direction:

1. Preheat the oven and pizza stone (if using) to 500°F. Dust a pizza peel with cornmeal (if using a pizza stone), or brush two baking sheets with olive oil.

2. Roll out one of the dough balls to the desired size, and place it on the pizza peel (if using a pizza stone) or on the prepared baking sheet.

3. Sprinkle half of the spring garlic over the dough, then spread half of the Basil Pesto on top evenly. Sprinkle on half of the mozzarella, dot the pizza with half of the ricotta, and finish with half of the ham.

4. Transfer the pizza to the hot pizza stone or oven rack, and bake until the crust is golden and the cheese has melted, 5 to 7 minutes on the pizza stone or 7 to 10 minutes on the baking sheet.

5. Remove the pizza from the oven and transfer it to a cutting board. Let it rest for 5 minutes, then season with the salt and pepper. Slice and serve.

6. Repeat with the remaining dough ball and toppings.

Alsatian Bacon & Onion Pizza

MAKES 1 PAN PIZZA

PREP TIME: 10 minutes
COOK TIME: 20 minutes
TOTAL TIME: 35 minutes
Ingredients:

- ½ cup crème fraîche, at room temperature
- 1 cup fromage blanc, at room temperature
- ½ cup White Sauce
- 2 pinches ground nutmeg
- ½ pound slab bacon (lardons), chopped into bite-size pieces
- 1 medium white onion, sliced thin
- 1 teaspoon fine sea salt, divided
- No-Knead Pan Pizza Dough Freshly ground black pepper

Direction:

1. Preheat the oven to 500°F.

2. In a medium bowl, whisk together the crème fraîche, fromage blanc, White Sauce, and nutmeg until well blended.

3. In a large skillet over medium heat, cook the bacon, stirring occasionally, until lightly crisp, about 6 minutes. Using a slotted spoon, transfer the bacon to a paper towel–lined plate.

4. Add the onion to the skillet. Season with ½ teaspoon of salt and cook, stirring frequently, until translucent, about 5 minutes. The onions shouldn't take color but should be soft. Using a slotted spoon, transfer the cooked onion to a fine-mesh strainer and gently press out any excess fat.

5. Leaving a 1-inch border, spread the cheese mixture in a thin layer over the dough. Top with an even layer of onions and scatter on the bacon.

6. Transfer the pizza to the oven and bake until the crust is deeply golden, 8 to 10 minutes.

7. Remove the pizza from the oven and let it rest for 5 minutes, then season with the remaining ½ teaspoon of salt, and pepper. Slice and serve.

Prosciutto & Arugula Pizza

MAKES 2 (12- TO 14-INCH) PIZZAS OR 4 PERSONAL PIZZAS

PREP TIME: 10 minutes
COOK TIME: 20 minutes
TOTAL TIME: 35 minutes

Ingredients:

- Cornmeal or flour, for dusting
- 2 tablespoons extra-virgin olive oil, plus more for brushing
- Simply Amazing Pizza Dough or Pro Dough
- 1 cup New York–Style Pizza Sauce
- 8 slices prosciutto
- 6 ounces fresh mozzarella cheese, sliced or shredded
- 3 cups arugula

- ¼ teaspoon salt
- ⅛ teaspoon freshly ground black pepper
- 3 ounces Parmesan cheese, shaved with a vegetable peeler

Direction:

1. Preheat the oven and pizza stone (if using) to 500°F. Dust a pizza peel with cornmeal (if using a pizza stone), or brush two baking sheets with olive oil.

2. Roll out one of the dough balls to the desired size, and place it on the pizza peel (if using a pizza stone) or on the prepared baking sheet.

3. Leaving a 1-inch border, spread half of the sauce evenly onto the dough. Lay half of the prosciutto slices on top, then finish with half of the mozzarella.

4. Transfer the pizza to the hot pizza stone or oven rack, and bake until the crust is golden and the cheese has melted, 5 to 7 minutes on the pizza stone or 7 to 10 minutes on the baking sheet.

5. Remove the pizza from the oven and transfer it to a cutting board. Let it rest for 5 minutes, then top with half of the arugula, olive oil, salt, pepper, and Parmesan. Slice and serve.

6. Repeat with the remaining dough ball and toppings.

Pancetta, Egg & Spinach Pizza

MAKES 2 (12- TO 14-INCH) PIZZAS OR 4 PERSONAL PIZZAS

PREP TIME: 10 minutes
COOK TIME: 30 minutes
TOTAL TIME: 45 minutes

Ingredients:

- Cornmeal or flour, for dusting
- 1 tablespoon extra-virgin olive oil, plus more for brushing
- 3 ounces pancetta, finely diced
- 2 garlic cloves, minced
- 4 cups baby spinach, stems removed
- ¼ teaspoon salt
- Simply Amazing Pizza Dough or Pro Dough
- 1 cup New York–Style Pizza Sauce
- 1 cup grated fontina cheese
- 2 large eggs
- 2 tablespoons grated Parmesan cheese
- 2 tablespoons chopped fresh flat-leaf parsley
- ⅛ teaspoon freshly ground black pepper

Direction:

1. Preheat the oven and pizza stone (if using) to 500°F. Dust a pizza peel with cornmeal (if using a

pizza stone), or brush two baking sheets with olive oil.

2. In a large skillet over medium heat, cook the pancetta until crisp, about 5 minutes, turning frequently. Transfer to a paper towel–lined plate.

3. Discard the rendered fat from the skillet and add the olive oil. Return the skillet to medium heat and, when the oil begins to shimmer, add the garlic. Swirl the garlic in the pan for a minute, then add the spinach. Use tongs to turn the spinach, watching it decrease in volume. Cook the spinach for 2 to 3 minutes, until it's wilted but still has structure. Season with the salt and remove the skillet from the heat. Roughly chop the spinach.

4. Roll out one of the dough balls to the desired size, and place it on the pizza peel (if using a pizza stone) or on the prepared baking sheet.

5. Leaving a 1-inch border, spread the sauce evenly onto the dough.

6. Top with half of the fontina followed by half of the spinach. Crack one egg, positioning the yolk in the center of the pizza. (If using a pizza peel, I find it easier to transfer the pizza to the oven, pull the oven rack out, and then crack the egg over the top.) Sprinkle with half of the Parmesan.

7. Transfer the pizza to the hot pizza stone or oven rack, and bake until the crust is golden and the egg yolk holds its shape when jiggled, 5 to 7 minutes on the pizza stone or 7 to 10 minutes on the baking sheet.

8. Remove the pizza from the oven and transfer it to a cutting board. Let it rest for 5 minutes, then season with half of the parsley and black pepper. Slice and serve.

9. Repeat from step 4 with the remaining dough ball and toppings.

Chicken, Kale & Butternut Squash Pizza

MAKES 2 (12- TO 14-INCH) PIZZAS OR 4 PERSONAL PIZZAS

PREP TIME: 10 minutes
COOK TIME: 40 minutes
TOTAL TIME: 55 minutes
Ingredients:

- Cornmeal or flour, for dusting
- 3 tablespoons extra-virgin olive oil, divided, plus more for brushing and drizzling
- 2 cups diced butternut squash
- 1 fresh rosemary sprig, stemmed and chopped
- Salt
- Freshly ground black pepper
- 3 cups stemmed, roughly chopped kale
- 1½ cups shredded cooked chicken
- Simply Amazing Pizza Dough

- 1½ cups grated Gruyère cheese
- 3 tablespoons grated Asiago cheese
- 2 tablespoons toasted walnuts, roughly chopped

Direction:

1. Preheat the oven and pizza stone (if using) to 500°F. Dust a pizza peel with cornmeal (if using a pizza stone), or brush two baking sheets with olive oil.

2. In a medium skillet over medium-high heat, heat 1 tablespoon of olive oil. When it shimmers, add the butternut squash and rosemary. Season with salt and pepper. Cook the squash until tender and browned, about 20 minutes, stirring frequently.

3. In a large bowl, use your hands to toss the kale and shredded chicken with the remaining 2 tablespoons of olive oil, and season with salt and pepper.

4. Roll out one of the dough balls to the desired size, and place it on the pizza peel (if using a pizza stone) or on the prepared baking sheet.

5. Sprinkle half of the Gruyère over the dough and top with half of the kale and chicken, followed by half of the caramelized butternut squash and Asiago.

6. Transfer the pizza to the hot pizza stone or oven rack, and bake until the crust is golden and the cheese has melted, 5 to 7 minutes on the pizza stone or 7 to 10 minutes on the baking sheet.

7. Remove the pizza from the oven and transfer it to a cutting board. Let it rest for 5 minutes, then drizzle it with a little olive oil, season with salt and pepper, and sprinkle on half of the walnuts. Slice and serve.

8. Repeat from step 4 with the remaining dough ball and toppings.

Chicken, Pesto & Ricotta Pizza

MAKES 2 (12- TO 14-INCH) PIZZAS OR 4 PERSONAL PIZZAS

PREP TIME: 10 minutes
COOK TIME: 20 minutes
TOTAL TIME: 35 minutes

Ingredients:

- Cornmeal or flour, for dusting
- 2 tablespoons extra-virgin olive oil, plus more for brushing
- Simply Amazing Pizza Dough or Pro Dough
- 2 cups whole-milk ricotta cheese
- 1 cup Basil Pesto
- 2 cups shredded cooked chicken
- 2 plum tomatoes, sliced thin
- ¼ cup freshly grated pecorino romano cheese

- ⅛ teaspoon freshly ground black pepper, plus more for finishing

Direction:

1. Preheat the oven and pizza stone (if using) to 500°F. Dust a pizza peel with cornmeal (if using a pizza stone), or brush two baking sheets with olive oil.

2. Roll out one of the dough balls to the desired size, and place it on the pizza peel (if using a pizza stone) or on the prepared baking sheet.

3. Spoon half of the ricotta in dollops onto the dough and spread it into a thin, even layer. Spoon half of the Basil Pesto on top of the ricotta, spread it out, and sprinkle on half of the shredded chicken and tomato slices. Drizzle with half of the olive oil, sprinkle with half of the pecorino romano, and season with half of the black pepper.

4. Transfer the pizza to the hot pizza stone or oven rack, and bake until the crust is golden and the cheese has melted, 5 to 7 minutes on the pizza stone or 7 to 10 minutes on the baking sheet.

5. Remove the pizza from the oven and transfer it to a cutting board. Let it rest for 5 minutes, then season with another grind or two of black pepper. Slice and serve.

6. Repeat with the remaining dough ball and toppings.

Grilled Clam & Corn Pizza

MAKES 2 (12- TO 14-INCH) PIZZAS OR 4 PERSONAL PIZZAS

PREP TIME: 15 minutes
COOK TIME: 30 minutes
TOTAL TIME: 45 minutes

Ingredients:

- 6 ears corn, shucked
- 1 tablespoon extra-virgin olive oil, plus more for drizzling
- 2 dozen littleneck clams, scrubbed
- Simply Amazing Pizza Dough or Pro Dough
- 2 pinches red pepper flakes
- 3 tablespoons chopped fresh flat-leaf parsley

Direction:

1. Preheat a grill to indirect high heat or a grill pan to high heat.

2. Rub the corn with the olive oil and grill over direct high heat for 5 minutes, turning every minute or two, until lightly charred on all sides. Remove the corn from the heat and cut the kernels from the cobs into a large bowl.

3. In a large pot with a lid, bring 1 inch of water to a boil over high heat. Add the clams, cover, and cook for 3 to 5 minutes, or until the clams open. Loosen the clams from their shells, and transfer to a

medium bowl. Discard the shells and any clams that did not open.

4. Roll out one of the dough balls to the desired size.

5. Grill the dough on each side for 2 to 3 minutes, remove from the heat, and top with half of the grilled corn and steamed clams. Season with a pinch of red pepper flakes and a drizzle of olive oil. Return the pizza to the grill, cover, and grill until the crust is well browned, about 5 minutes.

6. Transfer to a cutting board and sprinkle with half of the chopped parsley. Slice and serve.

7. Repeat from step 4 with the remaining dough ball and toppings.

Fig, Prosciutto & Goat Cheese Pizza

MAKES 2 (12- TO 14-INCH) PIZZAS OR 4 PERSONAL PIZZAS

PREP TIME: 10 minutes
COOK TIME: 20 minutes
TOTAL TIME: 35 minutes
Ingredients:

- Cornmeal or flour, for dusting
- 2 tablespoons extra-virgin olive oil, plus more for brushing
- Simply Amazing Pizza Dough or Pro Dough
- ¼ cup fig jam
- ½ cup shredded mozzarella cheese
- ½ cup crumbled goat cheese
- 8 slices prosciutto
- 8 figs, stemmed and quartered
- 4 fresh thyme sprigs, stemmed
- ¼ teaspoon fine sea salt
- ⅛ teaspoon freshly ground black pepper

Direction:

1. Preheat the oven and pizza stone (if using) to 500°F. Dust a pizza peel with cornmeal (if using a pizza stone), or brush two baking sheets with olive oil.

2. Roll out one of the dough balls to the desired size, and place it on the pizza peel (if using a pizza stone) or on the prepared baking sheet.

3. Leaving a 1-inch border, spoon half of the fig jam evenly onto the dough. Top with half of the mozzarella, goat cheese, and prosciutto. Arrange half of the figs on the pizza, sprinkle on half of the thyme, and season with half of the salt and pepper.

4. Transfer the pizza to the hot pizza stone or oven rack, and bake until the crust is golden and the cheese has melted, 5 to 7 minutes on the pizza stone or 7 to 10 minutes on the baking sheet.

5. Remove the pizza from the oven and transfer it to a cutting board. Let it rest for 5 minutes, then drizzle with half of the olive oil. Slice and serve.

6. Repeat with the remaining dough ball and toppings.

Ricotta Margherita

MAKES 2 (12- TO 14-INCH) PIZZAS OR 4 PERSONAL PIZZAS

PREP TIME: 10 minutes
COOK TIME: 20 minutes
TOTAL TIME: 35 minutes

Ingredients:

- Cornmeal or flour, for dusting
- 1 tablespoon extra-virgin olive oil, plus more for brushing
- Simply Amazing Pizza Dough or Pro Dough
- 1 cup New York–Style Pizza Sauce
- 1 teaspoon dried oregano
- ½ cup fresh ricotta cheese
- 6 ounces fresh mozzarella cheese, sliced thin
- ¼ teaspoon fine sea salt
- ⅛ teaspoon freshly ground black pepper
- 8 fresh basil leaves, torn

Direction:

1. Preheat the oven and pizza stone (if using) to 500°F. Dust a pizza peel with cornmeal (if using a pizza stone), or brush two baking sheets with olive oil.

2. Roll out one of the dough balls to the desired size, and place it on the pizza peel (if using a pizza stone) or on the prepared baking sheet.

3. Leaving a 1-inch border, spoon half of the sauce onto the dough, spreading it evenly. Sprinkle on half of the oregano.

4. Spoon half of the ricotta cheese in small dollops all over the pizza, then arrange half of the mozzarella slices on top. Season with half of the salt and pepper, and scatter on half of the torn basil leaves.

5. Transfer the pizza to the hot pizza stone or oven rack, and bake until the crust is golden and the cheese has melted, 5 to 7 minutes on the pizza stone or 7 to 10 minutes on the baking sheet.

6. Remove the pizza from the oven and transfer it to a cutting board. Let it rest for 5 minutes. Slice and serve.

7. Repeat with the remaining dough ball and toppings.

Vegan Spinach & Mushroom Pizza

MAKES 2 (12- TO 14-INCH) PIZZAS OR 4 PERSONAL PIZZAS

PREP TIME: 15 minutes
COOK TIME: 30 minutes
TOTAL TIME: 50 minutes

Ingredients:

- Cornmeal or flour, for dusting
- 4 tablespoons extra-virgin olive oil, divided, plus more for brushing
- 2 cups sliced cremini mushrooms
- ½ teaspoon fine sea salt
- 1 garlic clove, minced
- ⅛ teaspoon red pepper flakes
- 4 cups baby spinach, stems removed
- Simply Amazing Pizza Dough or Pro Dough
- 1 cup New York–Style Pizza Sauce
- ½ cup grated vegan mozzarella or Cheddar cheese
- ½ cup Cashew Cheese or other nut-based non-dairy cheese
- ¼ cup sliced black olives
- ½ medium yellow onion, sliced thin

Direction:

1. Preheat the oven and pizza stone (if using) to 500°F. Dust a pizza peel with cornmeal (if using a pizza stone), or brush two baking sheets with olive oil.

2. In a large skillet over medium-high heat, heat 3 tablespoons of olive oil until it shimmers. Add the mushrooms and salt, and let the mushrooms sit undisturbed for 2 minutes. Give the pan a shake and continue cooking for 3 minutes more, stirring occasionally, until the mushrooms have taken color but are still firm and vibrant. Using a slotted spoon, transfer the mushrooms to a medium bowl.

3. Reduce the heat to medium, add the remaining 1 tablespoon of olive oil to the skillet, then add the garlic and red pepper flakes. Swirl the skillet to flavor the oil, then add the spinach. Use tongs to turn the spinach, watching it decrease in volume. Cook the spinach for 2 to 3 minutes, until it's wilted but still has structure. Remove the skillet from the heat.

4. Roll out one of the dough balls to the desired size, and place it on the pizza peel (if using a pizza stone) or on the prepared baking sheet.

5. Leaving a 1-inch border, spoon half of the sauce onto the dough, spreading it evenly. Top with half of the vegan mozzarella and Cashew Cheese. Scatter half of the spinach and mushrooms over the pizza, followed by half of the black olives and sliced onion.

6. Transfer the pizza to the hot pizza stone or oven rack, and bake until the crust is golden and the cheese has melted, 5 to 7 minutes on the pizza stone or 7 to 10 minutes on the baking sheet.

7. Remove the pizza from the oven and transfer it to a cutting board. Let it rest for 5 minutes. Slice and serve.

8. Repeat with the remaining dough ball and toppings.

Beet, Pistachio & Watercress Salad

SERVES 4

PREP TIME: 10 minutes
COOK TIME: 1 hour
TOTAL TIME: 1 hour, 10 minutes
Ingredients:

For the beets
- 4 beets
- 3 tablespoons extra-virgin olive oil
- ½ teaspoon salt
- ¼ teaspoon freshly ground black pepper

For the dressing and the salad
2 tablespoons red wine vinegar
- ¼ cup extra-virgin olive oil
- 1 teaspoon ground cumin
- 1 teaspoon honey
- 1 teaspoon Dijon mustard
- 2 teaspoons sparkling water
- ¼ teaspoon salt
- Pinch freshly ground black pepper
- 2 fresh thyme sprigs, stemmed
- 4 cups watercress, rinsed and spun dry
- ½ cup roughly chopped pistachio nuts
- 2 ounces ricotta salata cheese, sliced

Direction:

To make the beets

1. Preheat the oven to 450°F.

2. Rinse and dry the beets, trimming the stem ends. Place each beet on a square of aluminum foil, drizzle with the olive oil, and season with the salt and pepper. Wrap the beets in their foil, place on a baking sheet, and bake until easily pierced with the tip of a knife, about 1 hour.

To make the dressing and the salad

1. Meanwhile, in a jar, combine the vinegar, olive oil, cumin, honey, mustard, and sparkling water. Shake before using.

2. Remove the beets from the foil and, when ready to use, rub the skins from the beets. Cut into a medium-size dice.

3. In a mixing bowl, spoon 2 tablespoons of dressing over the beets and lightly toss. Season with the salt, pepper, and thyme.

4. When ready to serve, in a salad bowl, toss the watercress with the dressing. Divide the watercress among 4 serving bowls and top with the diced roasted beets. Sprinkle each with pistachios and a slice of ricotta salata.

Roasted Cauliflower with Marcona Almonds & Parsley

SERVES 4

PREP TIME: 10 minutes
COOK TIME: 25 minutes
TOTAL TIME: 35 minutes

Ingredients:

- ½ cup Marcona almonds
- 1 head cauliflower, cut into florets
- ¼ cup plus 3 tablespoons extra-virgin olive oil, divided
- ½ teaspoon salt
- ¼ teaspoon freshly ground black pepper
- 1 cup flat-leaf parsley leaves (tightly packed)
- 1½ tablespoons balsamic vinegar
- 2 teaspoons freshly squeezed lemon juice

Direction:

1. Preheat the oven to 200°F.

2. Place the nuts on a baking sheet, and lightly toast for 3 to 4 minutes, until they are aromatic. Let cool and roughly chop.

3. Raise the oven temperature to 450°F.

4. Spread the cauliflower florets on a foil-lined baking sheet. Drizzle 3 tablespoons of olive oil over them and toss to coat. Season with the salt and pepper.

5. Roast the cauliflower until tender and golden, about 20 minutes, tossing the florets twice during the cooking process. Let cool to room temperature.

6. In a salad bowl, toss to combine the cauliflower, chopped nuts, and parsley leaves.

7. In a small bowl, whisk the remaining ¼ cup of olive oil, balsamic vinegar, and lemon juice together. Dress the salad just before serving.

Simply Amazing Pizza Dough

MAKES 2 (12- TO 14-INCH) PIZZAS OR 4 PERSONAL PIZZAS

PREP TIME: 15 minutes
RISE TIME: 45 minutes
COOK TIME: None
Ingredients:

- 1 package active dry yeast
- 1½ cups warm water (about 110 ° F)
- 2 tablespoons extra-virgin olive oil
- 4 cups all-purpose flour, plus more for dusting
- 1½ teaspoons salt

Direction:

1. In a medium bowl, add the yeast to the warm water and let bloom for about 10 minutes. Add the olive oil.

2. In a food processor or standing mixer fitted with a paddle attachment, pulse to blend the flour and salt. With the machine running, add the yeast mixture in a slow, steady stream, mixing just until the dough comes together. Turn the dough out onto a well-floured board, and with lightly floured hands, knead the dough using the heels of your hands, pushing the dough and then folding it over. Shape it into a ball, then cut it into 2 or 4 equal pieces.

3. Place the balls of dough on a lightly floured baking sheet and cover with a clean dishtowel. Let them rise in a warm, draft-free spot until they are doubled in size, about 45 minutes.

4. Proceed with the desired recipe.

Pro Dough

MAKES 2 (12- TO 14-INCH) PIZZAS OR 4 PERSONAL PIZZAS

PREP TIME: 40 minutes
RISE TIME: 6 hours, plus overnight
COOK TIME: None
Ingredients:

- ¼ teaspoon active dry yeast
- 1½ cups warm water
- 4 cups "00" flour or all-purpose flour, plus more for dusting
- 2 teaspoons salt
- Extra-virgin olive oil, for greasing

Direction:

1. In a medium bowl, add the yeast to the warm water and let it stand for 10 minutes. While the yeast is

blooming, rinse the bowl of a standing mixer with hot water and dry thoroughly. It should be warm to the touch. In the warm mixing bowl, combine the flour and salt. Add the yeast mixture and mix on low speed with a dough hook for 2 minutes. Raise the speed to medium-low and continue to mix for about 10 minutes, until the dough is cohesive and smooth and has pulled away from the sides of the bowl.

2. Knead again on medium-low speed for an additional 10 minutes, or until the dough is soft and warm to the touch.

3. Transfer the dough to a large, lightly oiled bowl, rolling the dough to coat it on all sides. Cover with plastic wrap and refrigerate overnight.

4. The next day, transfer the dough to a lightly floured board and punch it down. Cut it into 2 or 4 equal pieces and shape into smooth balls. Lightly flour the balls, place them on a baking tray, and cover with a damp kitchen towel. Let the dough rise again in the refrigerator for at least 4 hours or overnight.

5. Remove the dough from the refrigerator, place on a lightly floured baking sheet, and cover with a damp kitchen towel. Let it rise for 1½ to 2 hours, until it is doubled in size.

6. Proceed with the desired recipe.

Whole-Wheat Pizza Dough

MAKES 2 (12- TO 14-INCH) PIZZAS OR 4 PERSONAL PIZZAS

PREP TIME: 15 minutes
RISE TIME: 1 hour
COOK TIME: None
Ingredients:

- 2 cups warm water (110 °F)
- 1 packet active dry yeast (2¼ teaspoons)
- 2 teaspoons sugar
- 4½ cups whole-wheat flour, divided, plus more for dusting
- 3 teaspoons salt
- 2 tablespoons extra-virgin olive oil
- 2 tablespoons honey

Direction:

1. In the bowl of a standing mixer fitted with a dough hook, stir together the water, yeast, and sugar. Let it stand for 10 minutes.

2. Turn the mixer on low, and slowly add 2¼ cups of flour and the salt, olive oil, and honey. When all the ingredients are combined, add the remaining 2¼ cups of flour, and raise the speed to medium. Mix for 3 minutes, until the dough has come together.

3. Turn the dough out onto a well-floured board. Knead, using the heels of your hands, pressing the dough away and then folding it over itself. Repeat several times, then divide the dough into 2 or 4 equal pieces. Shape into balls and place on a parchment-lined baking sheet. Cover with a clean kitchen towel and let them rise until nearly doubled in volume, 30 minutes to 1 hour.

4. Proceed with the desired recipe.

Gluten-Free Pizza Dough

MAKES 1 (12- TO 14-INCH) PIZZA

PREP TIME: 20 minutes
RISE TIME: 1½ hours
COOK TIME: 25 minutes
Ingredients:

- 2 large Idaho potatoes
- 1 cup warm water
- 2 teaspoons honey
- 1 package active dry yeast
- 1 cup rice flour
- ½ cup tapioca starch
- 2 teaspoons salt
- 1 egg white
- 1 tablespoon extra-virgin olive oil

Direction:

1. In a medium saucepan over medium-high heat, cover the washed and unpeeled potatoes with water and cook for 20 to 25 minutes, until easily pierced with a knife. Drain, cool, and remove the skin. Pass the potatoes through a ricer or grate using the large holes of a box grater.

2. In a medium bowl, stir together the warm water, honey, and yeast, and set aside for 5 minutes, until the yeast foams (if this doesn't happen, discard and begin again with new yeast).

3. In the bowl of a standing mixer fitted with the paddle attachment, combine the potatoes, rice flour, tapioca starch, and salt. Mix on medium speed until the mixture forms a coarse meal. (Before adding the wet ingredients, use a bit of this mixture to lightly flour a surface for use in step 5.) Add the egg white and oil, then add the yeast mixture in a slow, steady stream. Continue mixing until the dough comes together.

4. Cover the bowl with plastic wrap, and set aside until the dough rises by half, 1 to 1½ hours.

5. Turn the dough out onto a lightly floured surface and divide it into 2 or 4 pieces; shape each piece into a ball. Roll out and proceed with the desired recipe.

No-Knead Pan Pizza Dough

MAKES 2 (13-BY-18-INCH) PIZZAS

PREP TIME: 5 minutes, plus 30 minutes to rest
RISE TIME: 8 to 18 hours
COOK TIME: None
Ingredients:

- 3½ cups bread flour, plus more for dusting
- ¼ teaspoon active dry yeast
- 1 teaspoon kosher salt
- ¾ teaspoon sugar
- 1⅓ cups warm water
- Extra-virgin olive oil, for drizzling

Direction:

1. In the bowl of a standing mixer fitted with the paddle attachment, combine the flour, yeast, salt, and sugar. With the mixer on low, add the water and mix just until combined, about 3 minutes.

2. Cover the bowl with a towel and let the mixture rise at room temperature for 8 to 18 hours, or until it is doubled in volume.

3. Turn the dough onto a well-floured board and divide in half. Lightly drizzle two large (13-by-18-inch) sheet pans with olive oil, and spread to cover with a thin, even coating.

4. Stretch one piece of dough to the length of the pan, then place it in the center of one pan. Gently pull and stretch the dough to fit the width. If it resists, refrigerate the dough for 10 minutes. When the dough fits the pan, cover the pan with a damp kitchen towel and let it rest for 30 minutes at room temperature. Repeat with the second piece of dough and the second sheet pan.

5. Proceed with the desired recipe.

Cauliflower Pizza Dough

MAKES 1 (12- TO 14-INCH) PIZZA

PREP TIME: 15 minutes
RISE TIME: None
COOK TIME: 30 minutes
Ingredients:

- 1 head cauliflower, cut into florets
- ½ cup shredded mozzarella or Mexican-blend cheese
- ¼ cup grated Parmesan cheese
- ½ teaspoon dried oregano
- ¼ teaspoon salt
- ¼ teaspoon garlic powder
- 2 eggs, lightly beaten

Direction:

1. Preheat the oven to 400°F, and prepare a vegetable steamer.

2. Steam the cauliflower until fork tender, 6 to 8 minutes. When cool enough to handle, press the florets with paper towels to dry and remove as much moisture as possible.

3. Transfer the florets to a food processor and pulse just until the cauliflower resembles cooked rice, being careful not to let it liquefy.

4. Transfer the cauliflower "rice" to a large mixing bowl. (The cauliflower should be as dry as possible, so it might be necessary to press it again with paper towels.) Add the mozzarella, Parmesan, oregano, salt, garlic powder, and eggs. Stir well until fully combined and then transfer the mixture to a baking sheet. Spread the dough evenly into a circle and bake, untopped, for 20 minutes.

5. Remove the pizza crust from the oven, add toppings, and proceed with the desired recipe.

Focaccia

MAKES 1 (13-BY-18-INCH) FOCACCIA

PREP TIME: 10 minutes, plus 1 hour to rest
RISE TIME: 3 hours
COOK TIME: 50 minutes
Ingredients:

-   1 cup peeled and diced Yukon gold potatoes (2 medium potatoes)
-   4½ cups bread flour
-   1 packet active dry yeast
-   1 teaspoon sugar
-   1½ teaspoons kosher salt, divided
-   Extra-virgin olive oil, for greasing and drizzling

Direction:

1. In a medium saucepan over high heat, cover the potatoes with cold water. Bring to a boil and cook until the potatoes are easily pierced with a fork, about 10 minutes. Ladle 1 cup of the cooking water into a blender, then drain the potatoes well. Put the drained potatoes in the blender with the cooking liquid, and purée. Set the potato purée aside to cool slightly.

2. In the bowl of a standing mixer fitted with the paddle attachment, combine the flour, yeast, sugar, and 1 teaspoon of salt. Add the potato purée and mix on low until a sticky dough forms. Cover the bowl with a towel and let it sit in a warm place until the dough has tripled in volume, 2 to 3 hours.

3. Lightly oil a large (13-by-18-inch) rimmed baking sheet. Use a rubber spatula to scrape the dough out onto the baking sheet. Pull the dough into the shape of the baking sheet and, with lightly oiled hands, use your fingertips to continue to press, spread, and dimple the dough. Try to create a uniform thickness as the dough spreads toward the rim of the pan.

4. Cover the dough with a clean dish towel and let it rest at room temperature for 1 hour. Halfway through the resting time, position the oven rack in the center of the oven and preheat to 400°F.

5. Drizzle with olive oil and sprinkle with the remaining ½ teaspoon of salt. Bake the focaccia for 30 to 40 minutes, until the top is evenly golden, turning the pan halfway through the cooking time.

Deep-Dish Pizza Dough

MAKES 2 (12- TO 14-INCH) PIZZAS

PREP TIME: 15 minutes
RISE TIME: 1½ hours
COOK TIME: None
Ingredients:

- 1 packet active dry yeast
- 1½ cups warm water
- 1 teaspoon sugar
- 3½ cups all-purpose flour, divided, plus more for dusting
- ½ cup cornmeal
- 1 teaspoon salt
- ½ cup extra-virgin olive oil plus 2 tablespoons, divided

Direction:

1. In the bowl of a standing mixer fitted with a dough hook, stir together the yeast, water, and sugar. Let it stand for 5 minutes, until the mixture is foamy.

2. With the mixer on low, add 1½ cups of flour and the cornmeal, salt, and ½ cup of olive oil. Blend until the ingredients are smoothly incorporated.

3. Add the remaining 2 cups of flour, a quarter-cup at a time, until all is incorporated to form a sticky dough. Continue kneading for 3 to 5 minutes, until a smooth dough forms.

4. Turn the dough out onto a lightly floured surface, and divide into 2 equal pieces. Shape each piece into a ball.

5. Lightly coat a large bowl with the remaining 2 tablespoons of oil. Place the dough in the bowl, turn it to oil on all sides, and let it rise in a warm place until almost doubled, 1 to 1½ hours.

Italian-Herbed Pizza Dough

MAKES 2 (12- TO 14-INCH) PIZZAS OR 4 PERSONAL PIZZAS

PREP TIME: 15 minutes
RISE TIME: 1½ hours
COOK TIME: None
Ingredients:

- 1 package active dry yeast
- 1½ cups warm water (about 110°F)
- 2 tablespoons extra-virgin olive oil
- 3 garlic cloves, minced
- 1 teaspoon dried oregano
- ½ teaspoon dried basil
- ½ teaspoon onion powder
- 4 cups all-purpose flour, plus more for dusting
- 1½ teaspoons salt

Direction:

1. In a medium bowl, add the yeast to the warm water and let bloom for about 10 minutes. Add the olive oil, garlic, oregano, basil, and onion powder.

2. In a food processor, pulse to blend the flour and salt. With the machine running, add the yeast mixture in a slow, steady stream. Turn the machine off as soon as the dough comes together. Turn the dough out onto a well-floured board and, with lightly floured hands, knead the dough using the heels of your hands, pushing the dough and then folding it over. Shape into a ball and cut into 2 or 4 pieces.

3. Place the balls on a lightly floured pan and cover with a kitchen towel. Let the dough rise until it doubles in volume, about 1½ hours.

New York–Style Pizza Sauce

MAKES 1 QUART

PREP TIME: 10 minutes
COOK TIME: 25 minutes
Ingredients:

- 2 tablespoons extra-virgin olive oil
- 1 small yellow onion, chopped (½ cup)
- 3 garlic cloves, smashed
- 1 (28-ounce) can whole peeled San Marzano tomatoes, undrained
- 1 teaspoon fine sea salt
- ⅛ teaspoon freshly ground black pepper
- 1 to 2 tablespoons sugar

Direction:

1. In a large saucepan over medium-high heat, heat the olive oil until it shimmers. Reduce the heat to medium and add the chopped onion. Cook, stirring occasionally, for 5 minutes. Add the garlic and continue to cook for 2 to 3 minutes more, until the onion is translucent and the garlic is aromatic.

2. Add the tomatoes and their juice, and bring to a simmer, stirring occasionally with a wooden spoon to break them apart. Simmer for 10 to 15 minutes, until the sauce has thickened.

3. Using an immersion blender or food processor, pulse until the sauce is smooth. Season with the salt, pepper, and sugar.

No-Cook Pizza Sauce

MAKES 1 QUART

PREP TIME: 10 minutes
COOK TIME: None
Ingredients:

- 1 (28-ounce) can whole peeled San Marzano tomatoes, undrained
- 6 garlic cloves, chopped
- 2 teaspoons balsamic vinegar
- ½ teaspoon fine sea salt
- ⅛ teaspoon freshly ground black pepper
- 2 teaspoons extra-virgin olive oil

Direction:

1. In the work bowl of a food processor, purée the tomatoes and their juice together with the garlic, vinegar, salt, pepper, and olive oil until smooth, stopping to scrape down the bowl as necessary.

White Sauce

MAKES 2 CUPS

PREP TIME: 5 minutes
COOK TIME: 20 minutes
Ingredients:

- 3 tablespoons unsalted butter
- 3 tablespoons all-purpose flour
- 2 cups whole milk, heated until warm but not hot
- ½ teaspoon salt
- ⅛ teaspoon freshly ground black pepper

Direction:

1. In a medium saucepan over medium heat, melt the butter. When it foams, add the flour and whisk to form a smooth paste. Continue to cook for 5 minutes, stirring frequently, until the mixture deepens in color.

2. Add the heated milk in half-cup increments, whisking in each to incorporate and cooking briefly before adding the next. When all the milk has been added, raise the heat to medium-high and continue whisking until the thickened sauce just begins to bubble, about 10 minutes. Remove from the heat.

3. Season with the salt and pepper. Keep at room temperature if using, or refrigerate if making ahead.

Cashew Cheese

MAKES 1½ CUPS

PREP TIME: 25 minutes to 1 hour
COOK TIME: None
Ingredients:

- 1 cup raw cashews
- ¼ cup water
- ¼ cup nutritional yeast
- 2 tablespoons freshly squeezed lemon juice
- 2 garlic cloves, peeled
- 1 tablespoon Dijon mustard

Direction:

1. In a medium bowl, soak the cashews in the water for at least 20 minutes, or up to an hour.

2. In a blender, purée the soaked cashews and their liquid together with the yeast, lemon juice, garlic, and mustard. Blend until thick, creamy, and, depending on your preference, smooth.

Basil Pesto

MAKES 2 CUPS

PREP TIME: 10 minutes
COOK TIME: None
Ingredients:

- ¼ cup extra-virgin olive oil, plus more for covering
- ¼ cup walnuts
- 2 tablespoons pine nuts
- ½ garlic clove
- ¼ teaspoon salt
- 2 cups tightly packed fresh basil leaves, washed and dried
- ½ cup finely grated Parmesan cheese
- 1 tablespoon butter, at room temperature

Direction:

1. In a food processor or blender, pulse to combine the olive oil, walnuts, pine nuts, garlic, and salt until smooth, stopping the machine as necessary to scrape down.

2. Add the basil in small handfuls, pulsing after each addition until smooth. When all of the basil has been incorporated, transfer to a medium mixing bowl. Add the grated Parmesan and the butter, mixing well to combine.

3. Cover with half an inch of extra-virgin olive oil, and store, refrigerated, for up to 3 days. Let come to

room temperature before using.

Black Olive Tapenade

MAKES 1½ CUPS

PREP TIME: 4 minutes
COOK TIME: None
Ingredients:

- ½ pound black Gaeta olives, pitted
- 2 tablespoons capers, drained
- 1 garlic clove, peeled
- Pinch red pepper flakes
- ¼ cup extra-virgin olive oil

Direction:

1. In a food processor or blender, pulse the olives, capers, garlic, and red pepper flakes until blended. Add the olive oil and pulse to form a coarse paste.

2. Refrigerate, covered, for up to a week.

Balsamic-Roasted Garlic

MAKES 1 CUP

PREP TIME: 10 minutes
COOK TIME: 40 minutes
Ingredients:

- Cloves from 3 heads garlic, peeled (about 2 cups)
- ½ cup balsamic vinegar
- 2 tablespoons extra-virgin olive oil
- 1 tablespoon water

Direction:

1. Preheat the oven to 350°F. Line a baking sheet with aluminum foil.

2. Spread the peeled garlic cloves on the prepared baking sheet.

3. In a small bowl, mix the balsamic vinegar, olive oil, and water. Spoon half of the mixture over the garlic cloves, tossing them to coat.

4. Bake for 30 minutes, stirring occasionally. Spoon the remaining vinegar mixture over the garlic and bake for 10 minutes more.

5. Refrigerate the garlic in an airtight container for up to 5 days. Bring to room temperature before

using.

Quick-Pickled Red Onions

MAKES 2 CUPS

PREP TIME: 10 minutes, plus 1 hour to rest
COOK TIME: None
Ingredients:

- ½ cup apple cider vinegar
- 1 tablespoon sugar
- ½ teaspoon salt
- 1 large red onion, halved lengthwise and cut into thin half moons

Direction:

1. In a large jar or other container with a lid, combine the vinegar, sugar, and salt. Stir until the sugar and salt are dissolved, then add the onions, pushing them down until they are completely submerged in the liquid.

2. Seal the container and let it rest at room temperature for at least 1 hour before using or refrigerating.

Sweet Onion Jam

MAKES 1½ CUPS

PREP TIME: 10 minutes
COOK TIME: 25 minutes
Ingredients:

¼ cup extra-virgin olive oil
3 large Vidalia or yellow onions, halved lengthwise and cut into half moons
¼ teaspoon salt
⅛ teaspoon freshly ground black pepper
¾ cup white balsamic vinegar
Direction:

1. In a large sauté pan over medium-high heat, heat the oil until it shimmers.

2. Add the onions, toss well to coat, and season with the salt and pepper. Reduce the heat to medium and cook, stirring frequently, until the onions are golden brown, 15 to 20 minutes.

3. Add the vinegar and raise the heat to medium-high to bring the liquid to a simmer. Cook, stirring frequently, until the vinegar has almost entirely evaporated, about 4 minutes.

4. Cool, transfer to a jar, and refrigerate for up to 3 days.

Oven-Roasted Cherry Tomatoes

MAKES 2 CUPS

PREP TIME: 5 minutes
COOK TIME: 30 minutes
Ingredients:

- 3 tablespoons extra-virgin olive oil
- 3 pints cherry tomatoes
- 3 garlic cloves, peeled
- 2 fresh thyme sprigs, stemmed
- 2 tablespoons chopped fresh basil
- ½ teaspoon salt
- ¼ teaspoon freshly ground black pepper

Direction:

1. Preheat the oven to 400°F.

2. On a parchment-lined baking sheet, toss the olive oil, cherry tomatoes, garlic, thyme, and basil. Season with the salt and pepper.

3. Bake for 30 minutes, gently tossing the tomatoes halfway through.

4. Scrape the roasted tomatoes into a large bowl, and stir until they form a chunky sauce.

5. The tomatoes can be refrigerated in an airtight container for up to 1 day.

Peperonata

MAKES 1½ CUPS

PREP TIME: 10 minutes
COOK TIME: 25 minutes
Ingredients:

- 4 red bell peppers, cut into 1-inch dice
- 2 tablespoons extra-virgin olive oil
- 2 tablespoons balsamic vinegar
- 2 teaspoons dried thyme
- Pinch red pepper flakes
- ¼ teaspoon salt

Direction:

1. Preheat the oven to 350°F.

2. In a large bowl, toss the bell peppers, olive oil, vinegar, thyme, red pepper flakes, and salt to coat.

3. Transfer to a rimmed baking sheet or a 9-inch ovenproof skillet, and bake for 25 minutes, stirring with a spatula every 5 minutes, until the peppers are soft and tender.

4. Remove the baking sheet or skillet from the oven and transfer the peperonata to a bowl; let it cool to room temperature before using.

5. The peperonata can be refrigerated in an airtight container for up to 3 days.

Chili Oil

MAKES 1 CUP

PREP TIME: 2 minutes
COOK TIME: 3 minutes
Ingredients:

- 1 cup extra-virgin olive oil
- 1 to 2 teaspoons red pepper flakes

Direction:

1. In a small saucepan over medium-low heat, heat the olive oil and red pepper flakes for 3 minutes. Remove the pan from the heat and let the oil cool to room temperature.

2. Transfer the cooled oil to a squeeze bottle or a clean jar with a lid. Refrigerate for up to 1 month.

Asparagus, Cherry Tomato & Pine Nut Pizza

MAKES 2 (12- TO 14-INCH) PIZZAS OR 4 PERSONAL PIZZAS

PREP TIME: 10 minutes
COOK TIME: 30 minutes
TOTAL TIME: 45 minutes
Ingredients:

- Cornmeal or flour, for dusting
- 1 tablespoon extra-virgin olive oil, plus more for brushing
- ¼ teaspoon salt, plus more for seasoning
- 1 bunch asparagus, tough ends snapped off and discarded
- ¼ cup pine nuts
- ⅛ teaspoon freshly ground black pepper
- Simply Amazing Pizza Dough
- 8 ounces fresh mozzarella cheese, shredded
- 1 cup Oven-Roasted Cherry Tomatoes
- 12 fresh basil leaves, snipped with scissors

Direction:

1. Preheat the oven and pizza stone (if using) to 500°F. Dust a pizza peel with cornmeal (if using a

pizza stone), or brush two baking sheets with olive oil.

2. Bring a large pot of salted water to a boil. Blanch the asparagus for 3 minutes, and transfer to a large bowl of ice water to stop the cooking process. Cut the stalks into thirds on the diagonal. In a medium bowl, drizzle the cut asparagus with the olive oil, and season with salt and pepper.

3. In a small skillet over medium-low heat, toast the pine nuts until fragrant, about 2 minutes, swirling the pan frequently to prevent burning. Remove the skillet from the heat and set aside to cool.

4. Roll and stretch one of the dough balls to the desired size and place it on the pizza peel (if using a pizza stone) or on the prepared baking sheet. Transfer the dough to the pizza stone or oven rack, and bake for 2 to 3 minutes, until the dough just begins to brown at the edges. Transfer the dough to a cutting board, and flip it over.

5. Leaving a 1-inch border, spread half of the cheese over the browned side of the crust, followed by half of the Oven-Roasted Cherry Tomatoes and asparagus.

6. Return the pizza to the oven and bake until the crust is golden and the cheese has melted, 5 to 7 minutes on a pizza stone or 7 to 10 minutes on a baking sheet.

7. Transfer the pizza to the cutting board and top with half of the toasted pine nuts and snipped basil leaves. Let it rest for 5 minutes, then slice and serve.

8. Repeat with the remaining dough ball and toppings.

Simple Pepperoni Pizza

MAKES 2 (12-INCH) PIZZAS OR 4 PERSONAL PIZZAS

PREP TIME: 5 minutes
COOK TIME: 20 minutes
TOTAL TIME: 30 minutes
Ingredients:

- Cornmeal or flour, for dusting, or extra-virgin olive oil, for brushing
- Simply Amazing Pizza Dough
- 1 cup New York–Style Pizza Sauce
- 1 cup grated mozzarella cheese
- 6 ounces pepperoni, sliced thin
- ¼ teaspoon salt

Direction:

1. Preheat the oven and pizza stone (if using) to 500°F. Dust a pizza peel with cornmeal (if using a pizza stone), or brush two baking sheets with olive oil.

2. Roll out one of the dough balls and place it on the prepared peel or baking sheet.

3. Leaving a 1-inch border, spread half of the sauce evenly over the dough. Top with half the mozzarella and then half the pepperoni. Sprinkle with half the salt.

4. Transfer the pizza to the hot pizza stone or oven rack, and bake until the crust is golden and the cheese has melted, 5 to 7 minutes on the pizza stone or 7 to 10 minutes on the baking sheet.

5. Remove the pizza from the oven and transfer it to a cutting board. Let it rest for 5 minutes, then slice and serve.

6. Repeat with the remaining dough ball and toppings.

Sicilian Pizza

MAKES 1 (13-BY-18-INCH) PAN PIZZA

PREP TIME: 10 minutes
COOK TIME: 10 minutes
TOTAL TIME: 25 minutes
Ingredients:

- 2 cups New York–Style Pizza Sauce
- No-Knead Pan Pizza Dough
- 1½ cups grated mozzarella cheese
- ½ cup shredded provolone cheese
- 12 slices soppressata

Direction:

1. Preheat the oven to 500°F.

2. Leaving a 1-inch border, spread the sauce evenly onto the dough.

3. In a medium bowl, toss together the mozzarella and provolone cheeses; sprinkle this mixture over the pizza. Top with the soppressata, 4 slices across and 3 slices down, ensuring that each slice of pizza is topped with one.

4. Transfer the baking pan to the preheated oven, and bake until the crust is golden and the cheese has melted, 7 to 10 minutes, rotating the pan halfway through.

5. Remove the pizza from the oven and let it rest for 5 minutes.

6. Run a spatula around the edges of the pan to loosen the pizza, slice, and serve.

Sausage, Pepper & Onion Pizza

MAKES 2 (12-INCH) PIZZAS OR 4 PERSONAL PIZZAS

PREP TIME: 10 minutes

COOK TIME: 40 minutes
TOTAL TIME: 55 minutes

Ingredients:

- Cornmeal or flour, for dusting
- 3 tablespoons extra-virgin olive oil, plus more as needed
- ¾ pound sweet Italian sausage (3 sausages)
- 1 medium yellow onion, sliced
- 1 red bell pepper, cut into ½-inch strips
- 1 green bell pepper, cut into ½-inch strips
- 2 garlic cloves, minced
- ¼ teaspoon red pepper flakes
- Simply Amazing Pizza Dough or Pro Dough
- New York–Style Pizza Sauce
- 1⅓ cups grated mozzarella cheese
- 1 teaspoon fine sea salt
- ⅛ teaspoon freshly ground black pepper
- ½ teaspoon dried oregano

Direction:

1. Preheat the oven and pizza stone (if using) to 500°F. Dust a pizza peel with cornmeal (if using a pizza stone), or brush two baking sheets with olive oil.

2. In a large skillet over medium heat, heat the olive oil until it shimmers. Add the sausages and cook until they are browned on all sides and register 160°F on an instant-read thermometer, about 8 minutes total. Transfer to a cutting board.

3. Add the onion to the hot pan (adding more oil if necessary), and sauté over medium heat until translucent, about 4 minutes. Add the red and green bell peppers. Sauté the mixture until the onions turn golden, about 4 minutes more, and then add the garlic and red pepper flakes. Cook, stirring, for about 2 additional minutes to infuse the mixture with the garlic. Using a slotted spoon, transfer the mixture to a small bowl.

4. Cut the sausages into ¼-inch-thick slices.

5. Roll out one of the dough balls to the desired size, and place it on the prepared peel or baking sheet.

6. Leaving a 1-inch border, spread half of the sauce evenly over the dough. Sprinkle half of the grated mozzarella over the pizza and then arrange half of the sausage slices on top. Spread half of the peppers and onions evenly over all.

7. Bake until the cheese has melted and the crust has browned, 5 to 7 minutes on the pizza stone or 7 to 10 minutes on the baking sheet.

8. Transfer the pizza to a cutting board and season with the salt, pepper, and dried oregano. Let it rest for 5 minutes, then slice and serve.

9. Repeat with the remaining dough ball and toppings.

Spinach & Mushroom Pizza

MAKES 2 (12- TO 14-INCH) PIZZAS OR 4 PERSONAL PIZZAS

PREP TIME: 10 minutes
COOK TIME: 30 minutes
TOTAL TIME: 45 minutes
Ingredients:

Cornmeal or flour, for dusting
4 tablespoons extra-virgin olive oil, divided, plus more for brushing
2 cups sliced cremini mushrooms
¼ teaspoon fine sea salt
⅛ teaspoon freshly ground black pepper
1 garlic clove
Pinch red pepper flakes, plus more for seasoning
4 cups baby spinach, stems removed
Simply Amazing Pizza Dough or Pro Dough
1 cup New York–Style Pizza Sauce
1 cup grated mozzarella cheese
Direction:

1. Preheat the oven and pizza stone (if using) to 500°F. Dust a pizza peel with cornmeal (if using a pizza stone), or brush two baking sheets with olive oil.

2. In a large skillet over medium-high heat, heat 3 tablespoons of olive oil until it shimmers. Add the mushrooms and the salt, and let the mushrooms sit undisturbed for 2 minutes. Give the pan a shake and continue to cook for 3 minutes more, stirring occasionally, until the mushrooms have darkened in color but are still firm and vibrant. Season with the pepper and transfer to a medium bowl.

3. Reduce the heat to medium and add the remaining 1 tablespoon of olive oil, the garlic, and the red pepper flakes. Swirl the garlic and red pepper flakes to flavor the oil, then add the spinach. Use tongs to turn the spinach, watching it decrease in volume. Cook the spinach for 2 to 3 minutes, until it's wilted but still has structure. Remove the skillet from the heat.

4. Roll out one of the dough balls to the desired size and place it on the prepared peel or baking sheet.

5. Leaving a 1-inch border, spoon half of the sauce evenly over the dough, then sprinkle on half of the mozzarella. Scatter half of the spinach over the pizza, followed by half of the mushrooms. The toppings should intermingle. Season with freshly ground black pepper or more red pepper flakes as desired.

6. Transfer the pizza to the hot pizza stone or oven rack, and bake until the crust is golden and the cheese has melted, 5 to 7 minutes on the pizza stone or 7 to 10 minutes on the baking sheet.

7. Remove the pizza from the oven and transfer it to a cutting board. Let it rest for 5 minutes, then slice and serve.

8. Repeat with the remaining dough ball and toppings.

Hawaiian Pizza

MAKES 2 (12- TO 14-INCH) PIZZAS OR 4 PERSONAL PIZZAS

PREP TIME: 10 minutes
COOK TIME: 25 minutes
TOTAL TIME: 40 minutes
Ingredients:

- Cornmeal or flour, for dusting, or extra-virgin olive oil, for brushing
- 4 slices center-cut bacon
- Simply Amazing Pizza Dough or Pro Dough
- 1 cup New York–Style Pizza Sauce
- 1 cup grated mozzarella cheese
- ¼ pound smoked ham, cut into ½-inch dice
- 1 cup diced fresh pineapple
- 2 tablespoons grated Parmesan cheese

Direction:

1. Preheat the oven and pizza stone (if using) to 500°F. Dust a pizza peel with cornmeal (if using a pizza stone), or brush two baking sheets with olive oil.

2. In a medium skillet over medium heat, cook the bacon until crisp, 2 to 3 minutes per side. Transfer to a paper towel–lined plate to cool. Cut into bits.

3. Roll out one of the dough balls to the desired size and place it on the pizza peel (if using a pizza stone) or on the prepared baking sheet.

4. Leaving a 1-inch border, spread half of the sauce evenly onto the dough. Sprinkle on half of the mozzarella, followed by half of the ham, chopped bacon, pineapple, and grated Parmesan cheese.

5. Transfer the pizza to the hot pizza stone or oven rack, and bake until the crust is golden and the cheese has melted, 5 to 7 minutes on the pizza stone or 7 to 10 minutes on the baking sheet.

6. Remove the pizza from the oven and transfer it to a cutting board. Let it rest for 5 minutes, then slice and serve.

7. Repeat with the remaining dough ball and toppings.

Meatball Pizza

MAKES 2 (12- TO 14-INCH) PIZZAS OR 4 PERSONAL PIZZAS

PREP TIME: 10 minutes
COOK TIME: 25 minutes
TOTAL TIME: 40 minutes

Ingredients:

- All-purpose flour, for dusting and coating
- ½ pound ground pork
- ½ pound ground veal
- 1 cup ricotta cheese
- ¼ cup grated Parmesan cheese plus 2 tablespoons, divided
- 2 tablespoons finely chopped fresh flat-leaf parsley
- ¼ teaspoon salt, plus more for sprinkling
- ⅛ teaspoon freshly ground black pepper, plus more for sprinkling
- 2½ cups New York–Style Pizza Sauce divided
- 2 tablespoons olive oil, plus more for brushing
- Simply Amazing Pizza Dough
- 2 cups grated mozzarella cheese

Direction:

1. Preheat the oven and pizza stone (if using) to 500°F. Lightly flour a baking sheet.

2. In a large mixing bowl, use your hands to combine the ground pork and veal, ricotta, ¼ cup of Parmesan, and the parsley. Season with the salt and pepper, and mix again.

3. Form each meatball by rolling 1 heaping tablespoon of the meat mixture between your palms. Place the meatballs on the prepared baking sheet, lightly rolling each one in flour.

4. In a medium saucepan over medium heat, heat 1½ cups of sauce; let it come to a gentle simmer.

5. Meanwhile, in a large skillet over medium-high heat, heat the olive oil. When it shimmers, add the meatballs, cooking on all sides for about 3 minutes, until browned. As they brown, transfer the meatballs to the simmering sauce to finish cooking, about 5 minutes total.

6. Dust a pizza peel with cornmeal (if using a pizza stone), or brush two baking sheets with olive oil.

7. Roll out one of the dough balls to the desired size and place it on the pizza peel (if using a pizza stone) or on the prepared baking sheet.

8. Leaving a 1-inch border, spread ½ cup of the remaining sauce evenly onto the dough. Top the sauce with half of the mozzarella and half of the meatballs. Spoon a little extra sauce from the pan onto the pizza, and finish with 1 tablespoon of the remaining Parmesan cheese and a sprinkling of salt and pepper.

9. Transfer the pizza to the hot pizza stone or oven rack, and bake until the crust is golden and the cheese has melted, 5 to 7 minutes on the pizza stone or 7 to 10 minutes on the baking sheet.

10. Remove the pizza from the oven and transfer it to a cutting board. Let it rest for 5 minutes, then slice

and serve.

11. Repeat from step 7 with the remaining dough ball and toppings.

Four-Cheese Pizza

MAKES 2 (12- TO 14-INCH) PIZZAS OR 4 PERSONAL PIZZAS

PREP TIME: 15 minutes
COOK TIME: 20 minutes
TOTAL TIME: 40 minutes
Ingredients:

- Cornmeal or flour, for dusting, or extra-virgin olive oil, for brushing
- Simply Amazing Pizza Dough
- 1 cup New York–Style Pizza Sauce
- ¾ cup grated mozzarella or 6 ounces sliced fresh mozzarella cheese
- ¾ cup grated fontina cheese
- 2 plum tomatoes, sliced thin
- ⅓ cup crumbled goat cheese
- ½ cup Parmesan cheese
- 8 fresh basil leaves, torn or roughly chopped
- 1 tablespoon chopped fresh parsley
- ¼ teaspoon salt
- ⅛ teaspoon freshly ground black pepper

Direction:

1. Preheat the oven and pizza stone (if using) to 500°F. Dust a pizza peel with cornmeal (if using a pizza stone), or brush two baking sheets with olive oil.

2. Roll out one of the dough balls to the desired size, and place it on the pizza peel (if using a pizza stone) or on the prepared baking sheet.

3. Leaving a 1-inch border, spread half of the sauce evenly over the dough. Sprinkle on half of the mozzarella and fontina. Arrange half of the tomato slices on top, and finish with half of the goat cheese and Parmesan.

4. Transfer the pizza to the hot pizza stone or oven rack, and bake until the crust is golden and the cheese has melted, 5 to 7 minutes on the pizza stone or 7 to 10 minutes on the baking sheet.

5. Remove the pizza from the oven and transfer it to a cutting board. Let it rest for 5 minutes, then top with half of the basil and parsley and season with half of the salt and pepper. Slice and serve.

6. Repeat with the remaining dough ball and toppings.

Meat Lover's Pizza

MAKES 2 (12- TO 14-INCH) PIZZAS OR 4 PERSONAL PIZZAS

PREP TIME: 15 minutes
COOK TIME: 35 minutes
TOTAL TIME: 50 minutes
Ingredients:

- Cornmeal or flour, for dusting
- Extra-virgin olive oil, for brushing and drizzling
- 4 slices center-cut bacon
- 4 slices prosciutto, cut into strips
- ½ pound sweet or hot Italian sausage, casings removed
- Simply Amazing Pizza Dough or Pro Dough
- 1 cup New York–Style Pizza Sauce
- 1½ cups grated mozzarella cheese
- ¼ cup thinly sliced pepperoni or soppressata
- 2 tablespoons chopped fresh flat-leaf parsley
- ½ teaspoon fine sea salt
- ¼ teaspoon freshly ground black pepper

Direction:

1. Preheat the oven and pizza stone (if using) to 500°F. Dust a pizza peel with cornmeal (if using a pizza stone), or brush two baking sheets with olive oil.

2. In a medium skillet over medium heat, cook the bacon until crisp, 2 to 3 minutes per side. Transfer to a paper towel–lined plate and set aside to cool.

3. Add the prosciutto to the skillet and cook over medium heat for about 3 minutes, stirring constantly, until crisp. Transfer the prosciutto to the plate with the bacon. Chop the bacon and prosciutto into bite-size pieces.

4. If there's not enough bacon fat in the skillet to prevent sticking, add a drizzle of olive oil and return the skillet to medium heat. Add the sausage to the skillet and cook for about 5 minutes, stirring constantly and breaking it up with a wooden spoon, until no pink color remains. Use a slotted spoon to transfer the sausage to another paper towel–lined plate.

5. Roll out one of the dough balls to the desired size, and place it on the pizza peel (if using a pizza stone) or on the prepared baking sheet.

6. Leaving a 1-inch border, spread half of the sauce evenly onto the dough. Sprinkle on half of the mozzarella, then half of the sausage, bacon, and prosciutto. Finish with half of the pepperoni so that the meat forms a single, even layer.

7. Transfer the pizza to the hot pizza stone or oven rack and bake until the crust is golden and the pepperoni is sizzling, 5 to 7 minutes on the pizza stone or 7 to 10 minutes on the baking sheet.

8. Remove the pizza from the oven and transfer it to a cutting board. Let it rest for 5 minutes, then top

with half of the chopped parsley, salt, and pepper. Slice and serve.

9. Repeat from step 5 with the remaining dough ball and toppings.

Deep-Dish Pizza

MAKES 1 DEEP-DISH PIZZA

PREP TIME: 10 minutes, plus 10 minutes to chill
COOK TIME: 35 minutes
TOTAL TIME: 1 hour
Ingredients:

- 1 tablespoon extra-virgin olive oil, plus more for greasing and drizzling
- 1 pound sweet or hot Italian sausage, casings removed
- 1 tablespoon chopped fresh flat-leaf parsley
- All-purpose flour, for dusting
- Deep-Dish Pizza Dough
- ¾ pound mozzarella cheese, sliced
- 1 cup sautéed mushrooms (optional)
- 2 cups New York–Style Pizza Sauce
- 1 cup freshly grated Parmesan cheese
- ½ teaspoon dried oregano
- ½ teaspoon dried thyme
- ¼ teaspoon coarse sea salt
- ⅛ teaspoon freshly ground black pepper

Direction:

1. Preheat the oven to 425°F. Coat a 12-inch round cake pan or cast iron skillet with olive oil.

2. In a medium skillet over medium heat, heat the oil. Add the sausage and cook for about 5 minutes, stirring constantly and breaking it up with a wooden spoon, until no pink color remains. Use a slotted spoon to transfer the sausage to a paper towel–lined plate. Add the parsley and toss well to combine.

3. Place the dough on a lightly floured surface and roll it out into a 14-inch circle.

4. Transfer the dough to the prepared pan, stretching it so that its diameter exceeds the rim of the pan. If the dough shrinks after being stretched, place it in the refrigerator for 10 minutes. Continue stretching until the dough can be tucked into the crease of the pan and cover the sides, similar to pie dough. Pierce the dough in a few places with the tines of a fork, and refrigerate for 10 minutes.

5. Transfer the empty pizza crust to the preheated oven and bake for 10 minutes, or until it just begins to brown. Remove the crust from the oven.

6. Cover the bottom of the crust with the sliced mozzarella in an even layer. Spread the sausage-parsley mixture on top of the cheese, followed by the mushrooms (if using), and then the sauce. Sprinkle

with the Parmesan, oregano, and thyme, drizzle lightly with olive oil, and sprinkle with the salt and pepper.

7. Bake the pizza for 25 minutes, until the filling is bubbling hot. Remove it from the oven and let it rest for 5 minutes. Use two spatulas to lift it out of the pan, slice, and serve.

Roasted Corn & Smoky Eggplant Pizza

MAKES 2 (12- TO 14-INCH) PIZZAS OR 4 PERSONAL PIZZAS

PREP TIME: 25 minutes, plus 1 hour to preheat grill
COOK TIME: 35 minutes
TOTAL TIME: 2 hours, 5 minutes

Ingredients:

- 3 (10-ounce) eggplants, trimmed and peeled
- ¼ teaspoon salt, plus more for seasoning
- 3 tablespoons extra-virgin olive oil, divided
- 6 ears corn, shucked
- 2 garlic cloves, minced
- 4 fresh thyme sprigs, stemmed
- ⅛ teaspoon freshly ground black pepper, plus more for seasoning
- ¼ teaspoon Hungarian smoked paprika
- Simply Amazing Pizza Dough or Pro Dough
- ½ pint cherry tomatoes, halved
- 1 zucchini, ends trimmed, peeled, and thinly cut lengthwise into ribbons

Direction:

1. Prepare a charcoal or propane grill as described or use a grill pan on the stove.

2. Cut the eggplant lengthwise into ½-inch slices. Set a wire rack inside a rimmed baking sheet. Sprinkle the eggplant slices with the salt, and place them in a single layer on the prepared rack. Let them drain for 10 minutes. Pat them dry with paper towels.

3. Brush the eggplant slices with 2 tablespoons of olive oil, and grill them over high direct heat for 4 minutes per side. The eggplant slices should be lightly charred and tender. Return the grilled eggplant to the metal rack.

4. Rub the corn cobs lightly with the remaining 1 tablespoon of olive oil, and grill them for 3 to 4 minutes per side, until lightly charred. Using a chef's knife, cut the kernels away from the cob, catching them in a large bowl.

5. 5 Using two chef's knives, chop the grilled eggplant, minced garlic, and thyme. Chop until the eggplant is a chunky purée. Use the blade of a knife to slide the purée into a large bowl. Season with salt, the pepper, and the smoked paprika. (If you'd prefer to do this in a food processor, pulse to a rough paste.)

6. Roll out one of the dough balls to the desired size.

7. Grill the dough over indirect high heat for 2 to 3 minutes per side, or until lightly charred.

8. Using tongs, transfer the crust to a cutting board. Spread half of the eggplant mixture over the crust, and top with half of the grilled corn, half of the cherry tomatoes, and a few ribbons of zucchini. Season with salt and pepper.

9. Return the pizza to the grill over indirect high heat, close the lid, and grill for 5 to 7 minutes or until the crust is golden and the tomatoes have collapsed and started to bubble.

10. Remove the pizza from the grill, and let it rest for 5 minutes. Slice and serve.

11. Repeat from step 6 with the remaining dough ball and toppings.

Grilled Skirt Steak Caprese Pizza

MAKES 2 (12- TO 14-INCH) PIZZAS OR 4 PERSONAL PIZZAS

PREP TIME: 15 minutes, plus 8 hours to marinate
COOK TIME: 30 minutes
TOTAL TIME: 8 hours, 55 minutes
Ingredients:

For the steak
- 2 tablespoons Dijon mustard
- ½ cup extra-virgin olive oil
- ¼ cup Worcestershire sauce
- 3 tablespoons soy sauce
- 4 garlic cloves, smashed
- 1 pound skirt steak
- 2 fresh rosemary sprigs, stemmed
- 2 fresh thyme sprigs, stemmed
- ½ teaspoon salt
- ¼ teaspoon freshly ground black pepper

For the pizza
- Simply Amazing Pizza Dough or Pro Dough
- 2 pinches dried oregano
- 6 ounces fresh mozzarella cheese, grated
- 1 pound heirloom tomatoes, sliced thin
- 8 fresh basil leaves, torn
- 4 handfuls arugula
- 2 tablespoons extra-virgin olive oil
- ¼ teaspoon fine sea salt
- ⅛ teaspoon freshly ground black pepper

- To prepare the steak

Direction:

1. In a small bowl, whisk the mustard, olive oil, Worcestershire, soy sauce, and garlic until well combined.

2. Place the steak in a casserole dish, pour the marinade over it, and scatter on the rosemary and thyme. Cover and refrigerate for 8 hours or overnight, turning the meat once or twice.

3. Heat an outdoor grill or a grill pan on the stove to high heat. Remove the steak from the marinade and season on both sides with the salt and pepper. Grill the steak for 5 minutes per side for medium rare. Remove the steak from the grill, and transfer it to a cutting board. Let it rest for 5 to 10 minutes, then slice it thinly against the grain.

To make the pizza

1. Preheat an outdoor grill to indirect high heat, or preheat the oven and pizza stone (if using) to 500°F.

2. Roll out one of the dough balls to the desired size, and place it on the pizza peel (if using a pizza stone) or on the prepared baking sheet. If you're grilling the pizza, brown the dough on both sides.

3. Sprinkle the dough with half of the dried oregano, then top with half of the shredded fresh mozzarella followed by half of the tomato slices. Garnish with half of the torn basil leaves.

4. Transfer the pizza to the grill, hot pizza stone, or oven rack, and grill or bake until the crust is golden and the cheese has melted, 5 to 7 minutes on the grill or pizza stone or 7 to 10 minutes on the baking sheet.

5. Remove the pizza from the grill or oven and transfer it to a cutting board. Top the pizza with half of the arugula and sliced steak. Drizzle half of the oil over the pizza and sprinkle on half of the salt and pepper. Slice and serve.

6. Repeat from step 2 with the remaining dough ball and toppings.

Pulled Pork, Brussels Sprouts & Purple Cabbage Pizza
MAKES 2 (12- TO 14-INCH) PIZZAS OR 4 PERSONAL PIZZAS

PREP TIME: 15 minutes
COOK TIME: 8 hours, 30 minutes
TOTAL TIME: 8 hours, 50 minutes
Ingredients:

For the pulled pork
- 1 tablespoon chili powder
- 1 tablespoon fine sea salt

- ½ teaspoon cayenne pepper
- ½ teaspoon cumin
- 1 tablespoon packed brown sugar
- 1 (4-pound) boneless pork shoulder (or Boston butt)
- 2 medium yellow onions, sliced
- 4 garlic cloves, smashed
- 1½ cups low-sodium chicken broth
- 1½ cups barbecue sauce

For the pizza
- Cornmeal or flour, for dusting, or extra-virgin olive oil, for brushing
- 4 slices of center-cut bacon
- ½ pound Brussels sprouts, trimmed, leaves separated
- ¼ teaspoon fine sea salt
- ⅛ teaspoon freshly ground black pepper
- Simply Amazing Pizza Dough or Pro Dough
- ¼ cup barbecue sauce
- 1 cup grated fontina cheese
- 1 cup grated pepper Jack cheese
- ¼ cup Quick-Pickled Red Onions

Direction:

To make the pulled pork

1. In a small bowl, mix together the chili powder, salt, cayenne, cumin, and brown sugar. Pat the meat dry with paper towels and rub it all over with the spice mixture.

2. Place the onions, garlic, and chicken broth in a slow cooker and add the spice-rubbed pork. Cook on low for 6 to 8 hours; the meat should be tender and falling apart. When the meat is finished cooking, discard the cooking liquid. Place the meat in a large bowl and shred it using two forks. Then pour in the barbecue sauce and mix well until the shredded meat is fully coated.

To make the pizza

1. Preheat the oven and pizza stone (if using) to 500°F. Dust a pizza peel with cornmeal (if using a pizza stone), or brush two baking sheets with olive oil.

2. In a large skillet over medium-high heat, cook the bacon until crisp, about 7 minutes. Remove the skillet from the heat and transfer the bacon to a paper towel–lined plate. When the bacon is cool enough to handle, chop it into bitesize pieces.

3. Return the skillet to medium-high heat, add the Brussels sprout leaves, and season with the salt and pepper. Sauté for 3 to 5 minutes, or until wilted, then immediately remove the skillet from the heat and transfer the Brussels sprouts to a medium bowl. Add the bacon and toss well to combine.

4. Roll out one of the dough balls to the desired size, and place it on the pizza peel (if using a pizza

stone) or on the prepared baking sheet.

5. Leaving a 1-inch border, brush the crust with half of the barbecue sauce, spreading it into a thin, even layer.

6. In a medium bowl, mix together the fontina and pepper Jack cheeses. Sprinkle half of the cheese mixture over the pizza, then top with half of the pulled pork and half of the Brussels sprouts and bacon.

7. Transfer the pizza to the hot pizza stone or oven rack, and bake until the crust is golden and the cheese has melted, 5 to 7 minutes on the pizza stone or 7 to 10 minutes on the baking sheet.

8. Remove the pizza from the oven and transfer it to a cutting board. Let it rest for 5 minutes, then top with half of the Quick-Pickled Red Onions. Slice and serve.

9. Repeat from step 4 with the remaining dough ball and toppings.

Garden Pan Pizza

MAKES 1 PAN PIZZA

PREP TIME: 15 minutes
COOK TIME: 45 minutes
TOTAL TIME: 1 hour, 5 minutes
Ingredients:

- 2 red bell peppers, cut into strips
- 1 zucchini, trimmed and cut into ¼-inch rounds
- 1 yellow summer squash, trimmed and cut into ¼-inch rounds
- 1 medium red onion, sliced
- 10 ounces fingerling or red bliss potatoes, scrubbed and cut into ¼-inch slices
- 3 tablespoons extra-virgin olive oil
- 5 fresh thyme sprigs, stemmed
- ½ teaspoon fine sea salt
- ¼ teaspoon freshly ground black pepper
- 1 cup New York–Style Pizza Sauce
- No-Knead Pan Pizza Dough
- 1¼ cups grated fontina cheese
- 1½ cups arugula

Direction:

1. Preheat the oven to 450°F.

2. On a foil-lined baking tray, spread the bell peppers, zucchini, summer squash, onion, and potatoes. Drizzle with the olive oil, sprinkle on the thyme, and season with the salt and pepper. Toss well, then transfer the baking sheet to the oven and roast for about 30 minutes, stirring twice during cooking. The potatoes should be fork tender.

3. Remove the vegetables from the oven and set aside. At this point, they can be used immediately or cooled to room temperature and refrigerated overnight in an airtight container.

4. Raise the oven temperature to 500°F.

5. Leaving a 1-inch border, spoon the sauce onto the dough, spreading it evenly. Scatter the fontina cheese over the dough, followed by the roasted vegetables.

6. Bake the pizza until the cheese has melted and the crust is golden, about 15 minutes. Remove it from the oven and let it cool for 5 minutes, then top it with the fresh arugula. Slice and serve.

Roasted Cauliflower, Fontina & Mushroom Pizza

MAKES 1 (12- TO 14-INCH) PIZZA OR 2 PERSONAL PIZZAS

PREP TIME: 10 minutes
COOK TIME: 45 minutes
TOTAL TIME: 1 hour
Ingredients:

- 3½ tablespoons extra-virgin olive oil, divided, plus more for greasing
- ½ head cauliflower, cut into bite-size florets
- ½ teaspoon salt, divided
- ¼ teaspoon freshly ground black pepper, divided
- 3 cups assorted mushrooms (about 12 ounces), stemmed and cut into ¼-inch-thick slices
- 3 fresh thyme sprigs, stemmed
- Cauliflower Pizza Dough
- ½ cup No-Cook Pizza Sauce
- ½ cup crumbled fontina cheese
- 1 fresh oregano sprig, stemmed

Direction:

1. Preheat the oven to 450°F. Coat a baking sheet lightly with olive oil.

2. Spread the cauliflower on a second baking sheet, drizzle with 1½ tablespoons of olive oil, and toss by hand. Season with half of the salt and pepper. Transfer the baking sheet to the oven and roast the cauliflower until tender and lightly browned, about 20 minutes, stirring midway through. Remove from the oven and set aside to cool.

3. Meanwhile, in a large skillet over medium-high heat, heat the remaining 2 tablespoons of olive oil. Add the mushrooms, season with the thyme and remaining ¼ teaspoon of salt, and let the mushrooms sit undisturbed for 2 minutes. Give the pan a shake and continue cooking for 3 minutes more, stirring occasionally, until the mushrooms have taken color but are still firm and vibrant. Season with the remaining ⅛ teaspoon of pepper and, using a slotted spoon, transfer the mushrooms to a plate.

4. Pat the Cauliflower Pizza Dough onto the prepared baking sheet. Transfer the sheet to the oven and

bake the dough for 15 minutes, or until it begins to crisp at the edges. Remove the crust from the oven.

5. Leaving a 1-inch border, spoon the sauce onto the crust, spreading it evenly. Top with the fontina, roasted cauliflower, and sautéed mushrooms. Return the pizza to the oven and cook for 4 to 5 minutes, or until the cheese is melted and the crust is golden.

6. Remove the pizza from the oven and transfer it to a cutting board. Garnish with the oregano and let it rest for 5 minutes. Slice and serve.

Potato, Pesto & Garlic Pizza

MAKES 2 (12- TO 14-INCH) PIZZAS OR 4 PERSONAL PIZZAS

PREP TIME: 10 minutes
COOK TIME: 45 minutes
TOTAL TIME: 1 hour
Ingredients:

- Cornmeal or flour, for dusting
- 3 tablespoons extra-virgin olive oil, plus more for brushing and drizzling
- 6 medium Yukon gold potatoes, scrubbed
- 1 fresh rosemary sprig, stemmed
- Simply Amazing Pizza Dough or Pro Dough
- 1 cup Basil Pesto ¼ teaspoon salt
- ⅛ teaspoon freshly ground black pepper
- 4 to 6 cloves Balsamic-Roasted Garlic ,mashed

Direction:

1. Preheat the oven and pizza stone (if using) to 500°F. Dust a pizza peel with cornmeal (if using a pizza stone), or brush two baking sheets with olive oil.

2. In a heavy, ovenproof skillet, heat the oil. When it shimmers, add the potatoes and the rosemary. Cook until the potatoes are lightly browned on all sides, about 8 minutes total. Transfer the skillet to the oven and cook until the potatoes are tender but still hold their shape, about 15 minutes. Remove the skillet from the oven and set it aside to cool. When the potatoes are cool enough to handle, cut them into ½-inch slices.

3. Roll out one of the dough balls to the desired size, and place it on the pizza peel (if using a pizza stone) or on the prepared baking sheet.

4. Leaving a 1-inch border, spoon half of the Basil Pesto onto the dough, spreading it evenly. Top the pizza with half of the potato slices. Drizzle with a little olive oil and season with half of the salt and pepper.

5. Transfer the pizza to the hot pizza stone or oven rack, and bake until the crust is golden, 5 to 7 minutes on the pizza stone or 7 to 10 minutes on the baking sheet.

6. Remove the pizza from the oven and transfer it to a cutting board. Let it rest for 5 minutes, then spread half of the Balsamic-Roasted Garlic over the pizza. Slice and serve.

7. Repeat from step 3 with the remaining dough ball and toppings.

Rosemary & Pear Pizza

MAKES 1 (12- TO 14-INCH) PIZZA

PREP TIME: 15 minutes
COOK TIME: 20 minutes
TOTAL TIME: 40 minutes
Ingredients:

- ½ recipe Simply Amazing Pizza Dough
- 4 Bosc pears
- ½ lemon
- Zest of 1 orange
- 1 tablespoon chopped fresh basil leaves
- 1 teaspoon chopped fresh rosemary leaves
- 2 tablespoons sugar
- ⅛ teaspoon freshly ground black pepper
- 2 tablespoons extra-virgin olive oil

Direction:

1. Preheat the oven and pizza stone (if using) to 450°F.

2. On a baking sheet, roll out the pizza dough to form a 12- to 14-inch disc.

3. Peel, halve, and cut away the core of the pears. Slice each pear half into thin wedges. Squeeze lemon juice over the pears.

4. Arrange the pears, starting at the outer edge of the crust (leaving no border), in a spiral toward the center. Sprinkle the orange zest, basil, rosemary, sugar, and pepper over the pears. Drizzle with the olive oil.

5. Bake for 20 minutes, until the pizza appears golden and crisp.

6. Remove the pizza from the oven and let sit for 5 minutes. Slice and serve warm or at room temperature.

Roasted Eggplant, Smoked Mozzarella & Cherry Tomato Pizza

MAKES 2 (12- TO 14-INCH) PIZZAS OR 4 PERSONAL PIZZAS

PREP TIME: 10 minutes, plus 10 minutes to sit
COOK TIME: 30 minutes
TOTAL TIME: 50 minutes
Ingredients:

- Cornmeal or flour, for dusting
- Simply Amazing Pizza Dough
- ½ teaspoon salt
- 1 large eggplant, peeled and cut crosswise into ½-inch-thick slices
- ¼ cup extra-virgin olive oil, divided
- 6 ounces smoked mozzarella cheese, cut into ½-inch dice
- 14 cherry tomatoes, halved
- 1 tablespoon fresh oregano leaves, roughly chopped
- ¼ teaspoon fine sea salt
- ⅛ teaspoon freshly ground black pepper

Direction:

1. Preheat a grill to indirect high heat or a grill pan on the stove to high heat. Dust a pizza peel with cornmeal.

2. Roll out one of the dough balls to the desired size and place it on the pizza peel.

3. Salt both sides of the eggplant slices and place them on a metal rack set over a rimmed baking sheet. Let sit for 10 minutes to draw the moisture out. Pat the slices dry with a paper towel and brush them lightly with 3 tablespoons of olive oil.

4. Grill the eggplant slices until tender, 5 to 6 minutes per side. The grill should be hot enough to char the eggplant. Transfer the grilled eggplant slices to a cutting board and cut into a rough dice.

5. Grill the pizza dough on one side for 3 minutes, flip the dough, and then top the pizza with half of the eggplant, mozzarella, and tomatoes. Close the lid and grill the pizza until the crust is golden and the mozzarella has melted, about 7 minutes.

6. Transfer the pizza to a cutting board. Drizzle with half of the remaining olive oil and season with half of the oregano, sea salt, and pepper. Slice and serve.

7. Repeat with the remaining dough ball and toppings, skipping steps 3 and 4.

Chipotle–Black Bean Pizza

MAKES 2 (12- TO 14-INCH) PIZZAS OR 4 PERSONAL PIZZAS

PREP TIME: 15 minutes
COOK TIME: 30 minutes
TOTAL TIME: 50 minutes
Ingredients:

- Cornmeal or flour, for dusting
- 2 tablespoons extra-virgin olive oil, plus more for brushing
- ¼ teaspoon dried oregano
- 1 medium yellow onion, diced
- ½ teaspoon salt, plus more for seasoning
- 2 garlic cloves
- ⅛ teaspoon freshly ground black pepper, plus more for seasoning
- ¼ cup low-sodium vegetable broth
- 2 cups canned black beans, rinsed
- 2 chipotle chiles in adobo, chopped, plus 1 tablespoon of the adobo sauce
- Simply Amazing Pizza Dough
- 1 cup grated vegan mozzarella cheese
- 1 red bell pepper, diced
- 1 cup diced avocado
- ½ cup fresh cilantro leaves

Direction:

1. Preheat the oven and pizza stone (if using) to 500°F. Dust a pizza peel with cornmeal (if using a pizza stone), or brush two baking sheets with olive oil.

2. In a large skillet over medium-high heat, heat the olive oil and oregano. When it shimmers, add the diced onion and salt and cook, stirring occasionally, until the onions are soft and translucent, about 5 minutes. Add the garlic and cook 1 minute more, stirring to combine. Season with salt and add the pepper. Transfer to a small bowl.

3. Add the vegetable broth to the sauté pan, then add the black beans, chipotle chiles, and reserved adobo sauce. Bring to a simmer and begin to mash the beans using a potato masher or immersion blender until they form a rough paste (add more vegetable broth if necessary). Season with salt and pepper. Remove from the heat and set aside.

4. Roll out one of the dough balls to the desired size, and place it on the pizza peel (if using a pizza stone) or on the prepared baking sheet.

5. Leaving a 1-inch border, spoon half of the black beans onto the crust, spreading them evenly. Top with half of the mozzarella and red pepper.

6. Transfer the pizza to the hot pizza stone or oven rack, and bake until the crust is golden and the cheese has melted, 5 to 7 minutes on the pizza stone or 7 to 10 minutes on the baking sheet.

7. Remove the pizza from the oven, transfer it to a cutting board, and let it sit for 5 minutes. Top the pizza with half of the avocado, cilantro, and freshly ground black pepper. Slice and serve.

8. Repeat from step 3 with the remaining dough ball and toppings.

Mediterranean Pizza

MAKES 2 (12- TO 14-INCH) PIZZAS OR 4 PERSONAL PIZZAS

PREP TIME: 10 minutes
COOK TIME: 30 minutes
TOTAL TIME: 45 minutes
Ingredients:

- Cornmeal or flour, for dusting
- 3 tablespoons extra-virgin olive oil, plus more for brushing
- 1 small red onion, diced (½ cup)
- ¼ teaspoon salt
- ⅛ teaspoon freshly ground black pepper
- 3 garlic cloves, minced
- 4 cups spinach, stems removed
- ¾ cup chopped fresh mint
- Whole-Wheat Pizza Dough
- 8 ounces crumbled feta cheese
- ½ cup halved black olives, preferably Kalamata
- ½ teaspoon dried oregano

Direction:

1. Preheat the oven and pizza stone (if using) to 500°F. Dust a pizza peel with cornmeal (if using a pizza stone), or brush two baking sheets with olive oil.

2. In a large skillet over medium-high heat, heat the olive oil until it shimmers. Add the onions, season with the salt and pepper and cook until translucent, about 4 minutes. Lower the heat to medium and add the garlic. Cook until it's fragrant, about a minute more.

3. Add the spinach to the pan and use tongs to toss the leaves as they decrease in volume, about 4 minutes. Remove the pan from the heat and add the chopped mint.

4. Roll out one of the dough balls to the desired size, and place it on the pizza peel (if using a pizza stone) or on the prepared baking sheet.

5. Top the dough with half of the spinach mixture, then dot with half of the feta and olives.

6. Transfer the pizza to the hot pizza stone or oven rack, and bake until the crust is golden, 5 to 7 minutes on the pizza stone or 7 to 10 minutes on the baking sheet.

7. Remove the pizza from the oven and transfer it to a cutting board. Let it rest for 5 minutes, then top with half of the dried oregano; slice and serve.

8. Repeat from step 4 with the remaining dough ball and toppings.

Fennel & Fontina Pizza with Olive Tapenade

MAKES 2 (12- TO 14-INCH) PIZZAS OR 4 PERSONAL PIZZAS

PREP TIME: 10 minutes

COOK TIME: 35 minutes
TOTAL TIME: 50 minutes
Ingredients:

- Cornmeal or flour, for dusting
- 2 tablespoons extra-virgin olive oil, plus more for brushing
- 4 fennel bulbs, stems and fronds discarded
- ¼ teaspoon salt
- ⅛ teaspoon freshly ground black pepper
- Simply Amazing Pizza Dough
- 1 cup grated fontina cheese
- ¼ cup Black Olive Tapenade
- 1 tablespoon fresh marjoram or thyme leaves

Direction:

1. Preheat the oven and pizza stone (if using) to 500°F. Dust a pizza peel with cornmeal (if using a pizza stone), or brush two baking sheets with olive oil.

2. Cut the fennel bulbs into quarters, remove the cores, and cut each quarter into thin strips. Spread the strips on a sheet, drizzle lightly with the olive oil, and season with the salt and pepper. Roast for 15 minutes, until tender. Remove from the oven and set aside.

3. Roll out one of the dough balls to the desired size, and place it on the pizza peel (if using a pizza stone) or on the prepared baking sheet.

4. Sprinkle half of the fontina over the dough, and top with half of the roasted fennel. Spoon half of the Black Olive Tapenade in dollops over the surface of the pizza.

5. Transfer the pizza to the hot pizza stone or oven rack, and bake until the crust is golden, 5 to 7 minutes on the pizza stone or 7 to 10 minutes on the baking sheet.

6. Remove the pizza from the oven and transfer it to a cutting board. Let it rest for 5 minutes, then scatter half of the marjoram the over top. Slice and serve.

7. Repeat from step 3 with the remaining dough ball and toppings.

Spring Pea Pizza with Ramps, Mint & Ricotta

MAKES 2 (12- TO 14-INCH) PIZZAS OR 4 PERSONAL PIZZAS

PREP TIME: 10 minutes
COOK TIME: 25 minutes
TOTAL TIME: 40 minutes
Ingredients:

- Cornmeal or flour, for dusting
- 2 tablespoons extra-virgin olive oil, plus more for brushing

- ½ cup shelled fresh English peas (or frozen and thawed peas)
- 10 ramps
- ¼ teaspoon fine sea salt
- Simply Amazing Pizza Dough or Pro Dough
- ¾ cup ricotta cheese
- 2 tablespoons chopped fresh mint

Direction:

1. Preheat the oven and pizza stone (if using) to 500°F. Dust a pizza peel with cornmeal (if using a pizza stone), or brush two baking sheets with olive oil.

2. If using fresh peas, bring a large pot of salted water to a boil. Fill a large bowl with ice water. Blanch the peas for 1 minute then, using a slotted spoon, transfer them to the ice water. Drain and set aside.

3. Spread the ramps on a baking sheet, drizzle with the olive oil, and sprinkle with the salt. Roast for 5 minutes to wilt. Transfer to a cutting board and cut into thirds.

4. Roll out one of the dough balls to the desired size, and place it on the pizza peel (if using a pizza stone) or on the prepared baking sheet.

5. Spoon half of the ricotta in dollops all over the dough. Scatter on half of the peas, ramps, and mint.

6. Transfer the pizza to the hot pizza stone or oven rack, and bake until the crust is golden, 5 to 7 minutes on the pizza stone or 7 to 10 minutes on the baking sheet.

7. Remove the pizza from the oven, transfer it to a cutting board, and let it sit for 5 minutes. Slice and serve.

8. Repeat from step 4 with the remaining dough ball and toppings.

Zucchini & Pistachio Pizza

MAKES 2 (12- TO 14-INCH) PIZZAS OR 4 PERSONAL PIZZAS

PREP TIME: 15 minutes
COOK TIME: 30 minutes
TOTAL TIME: 50 minutes

Ingredients:

- Cornmeal or flour, for dusting
- 2 tablespoons extra-virgin olive oil, plus more for brushing
- 1 medium green zucchini, halved lengthwise and cut thinly into half-moons
- 1 medium yellow summer squash, halved lengthwise and cut thinly into half-moons
- ¼ teaspoon salt
- Simply Amazing Pizza Dough
- 1 medium red onion, sliced thin
- 1 teaspoon fresh thyme leaves

- ¼ teaspoon red pepper flakes
- 1 teaspoon freshly squeezed lemon juice
- ¼ cup shelled pistachios, toasted

Direction:

1. Preheat the oven and pizza stone (if using) to 500°F. Dust a pizza peel with cornmeal (if using a pizza stone), or brush two baking sheets with olive oil.

2. In a large strainer set over a large bowl, toss the zucchini and summer squash well with the salt, and let it sit for about 5 minutes. Use a kitchen towel to press and squeeze the liquid from the squash mixture, removing as much moisture as possible.

3. Roll out one of the dough balls to the desired size, and place it on the pizza peel (if using a pizza stone) or on the prepared baking sheet.

4. In a large mixing bowl, toss together the drained squash mixture, onion, thyme, red pepper flakes, olive oil, and lemon juice. Arrange half of the vegetables on the dough.

5. Transfer the pizza to the hot pizza stone or oven rack, and bake until the crust is golden and the cheese has melted, 7 to 10 minutes on the pizza stone or 12 to 15 minutes on the baking sheet.

6. Remove the pizza from the oven and transfer it to a cutting board. Let it rest for 5 minutes, then garnish with half of the toasted pistachios. Slice and serve.

7. Repeat from step 3 with the remaining dough ball and toppings.

Escarole & Radicchio Pizza

MAKES 1 PAN PIZZA

PREP TIME: 10 minutes
COOK TIME: 20 minutes
TOTAL TIME: 35 minutes

Ingredients:

- 1 head escarole, cored, center ribs removed, leaves chopped
- ½ head radicchio, sliced
- 1 small red onion, sliced thin
- 1 tablespoon extra-virgin olive oil
- ¼ teaspoon fine sea salt
- Pinch red pepper flakes
- No-Knead Pan Pizza Dough
- 6 slices provolone cheese
- ½ cup grated pecorino romano cheese
- ¼ cup walnuts, toasted

Direction:

1. Preheat the oven to 500°F.

2. Toss the escarole, radicchio, and red onion slices in a bowl with the olive oil. Season with the salt and red pepper flakes. Cover the dough with the slices of provolone. Top the pizza with the escarole mixture, spreading it into a thin, even layer. Sprinkle with the pecorino.

3. Transfer the pizza to the oven and bake until the crust is golden, about 20 minutes.

4. Remove the pizza from the oven and use a spatula to transfer it to a cutting board. Let it sit for 5 minutes. Top the pizza with a drizzle of olive oil and the toasted walnuts. Slice and serve.

Brussels Sprout, Mozzarella & Sage Pizza

MAKES 2 (12- TO 14-INCH) PIZZAS OR 4 PERSONAL PIZZAS

PREP TIME: 10 minutes
COOK TIME: 30 minutes
TOTAL TIME: 45 minutes
Ingredients:

- Cornmeal or flour, for dusting
- 2 tablespoons extra-virgin olive oil, plus more for brushing and drizzling
- 1 red onion, sliced
- ½ teaspoon fine sea salt, divided
- ⅛ teaspoon freshly ground black pepper
- Simply Amazing Pizza Dough or Pro Dough
- 6 ounces fresh mozzarella cheese, shredded
- 12 Brussels sprouts, shredded or finely sliced
- 8 sage leaves, rolled and sliced thin
- ¼ cup grated Parmesan cheese
- 2 pinches red pepper flakes

Direction:

1. Preheat the oven and pizza stone (if using) to 500°F. Dust a pizza peel with cornmeal (if using a pizza stone), or brush two baking sheets with olive oil.

2. Spread the onion on a sheet tray, drizzle with the olive oil, and toss to coat. Season with ¼ teaspoon of salt, and the pepper. Transfer the baking sheet to the oven and roast for 10 to 12 minutes, or until the onions are caramelized. Remove from the oven and set aside.

3. Roll out one of the dough balls to the desired size, and place it on the pizza peel (if using a pizza stone) or on the prepared baking sheet.

4. Top the dough with half of the mozzarella, Brussels sprouts, and roasted red onion. Sprinkle on the remaining ¼ teaspoon of salt, half of the sage, and half of the Parmesan, followed by a drizzle of olive oil and a pinch of red pepper flakes.

5. Transfer the pizza to the hot pizza stone or oven rack, and bake until the crust is golden and the cheese has melted, 5 to 7 minutes on the pizza stone or 7 to 10 minutes on the baking sheet.

6. Remove the pizza from the oven and transfer it to a cutting board. Let it rest for 5 minutes. Slice and serve.

7. Repeat from step 3 with the remaining dough ball and toppings.

Spinach & Gruyère Pizza with Chili Oil

MAKES 2 (12- TO 14-INCH) PIZZAS OR 4 PERSONAL PIZZAS

PREP TIME: 15 minutes
COOK TIME: 20 minutes
TOTAL TIME: 40 minutes
Ingredients:

- Cornmeal or flour, for dusting, or extra-virgin olive oil, for brushing
- Simply Amazing Pizza Dough
- 2 garlic cloves, minced
- ½ cup grated pecorino romano cheese
- ¾ cup grated Gruyère cheese
- ¾ cup shredded fresh mozzarella cheese
- 5 cups baby spinach leaves, stems removed
- ¼ teaspoon fine sea salt
- 2 tablespoons Chili Oil

Direction:

1. Preheat the oven and pizza stone (if using) to 500°F. Dust a pizza peel with cornmeal (if using a pizza stone), or brush two baking sheets with olive oil.

2. Roll out one of the dough balls to the desired size, and place it on the pizza peel (if using a pizza stone) or on the prepared baking sheet.

3. Scatter half of the garlic over the dough and sprinkle with half of the pecorino, Gruyère, and mozzarella cheeses.

4. Transfer the pizza to the oven and bake just until the cheese melts, 2 to 3 minutes.

5. Remove the pizza from the oven, top it with half of the spinach and salt, and drizzle with 1 tablespoon of Chili Oil. Return the pizza to the oven and bake for another 4 to 5 minutes, or until the spinach wilts and begins to char.

6. Remove the pizza from the oven and transfer it to a cutting board. Let it rest for 5 minutes, then slice and serve.

7. Repeat with the remaining dough ball and toppings.

Shaved Asparagus, Ricotta & Oven-Roasted Tomato Pizza

MAKES 2 (12- TO 14-INCH) PIZZAS OR 4 PERSONAL PIZZAS

PREP TIME: 15 minutes
COOK TIME: 1 hour
TOTAL TIME: 1 hour, 20 minutes

Ingredients:

For the oven-roasted tomatoes (can be made up to 3 days in advance)
- 4 tomatoes, cut into ¼-inch-thick slices
- ½ teaspoon salt
- 1 tablespoon extra-virgin olive oil
- 3 tablespoons balsamic vinegar, divided

For the pizza
- Cornmeal or flour, for dusting
- 1 tablespoon extra-virgin olive oil, plus more for brushing
- 1 pound asparagus, shaved into long ribbons with a vegetable peeler
- 1 lemon wedge, for squeezing
- ¼ cup grated Parmesan cheese
- ¼ teaspoon fine sea salt
- ⅛ teaspoon freshly ground black pepper
- Italian-Herbed Pizza Dough
- ½ cup ricotta cheese

Direction:

To make the oven-roasted tomatoes

1. Preheat the oven and pizza stone (if using) to 275°F. Line a baking sheet with foil.

2. Spread the tomatoes on the prepared baking sheet. Season with the salt, and drizzle with the olive oil and 1½ tablespoons of balsamic vinegar. Transfer to the oven and roast for 20 minutes, or until the tomatoes have collapsed. Drizzle the remaining 1½ tablespoons of balsamic vinegar over the tomatoes, and continue cooking for 20 minutes more, or until they are caramelized. Remove the baking sheet from the oven and transfer the tomatoes to a medium bowl.

To make the pizza

1. Increase the oven temperature to 500°F. Dust a pizza peel with cornmeal (if using a pizza stone), or brush two baking sheets with olive oil.

2. In a medium bowl, toss together the asparagus, olive oil, a squeeze of lemon juice, and the Parmesan. Season with the salt and pepper and toss well.

3. Roll out one of the dough balls to the desired size, and place it on the pizza peel (if using a pizza stone) or on the prepared baking sheet.

4. Spoon half of the ricotta cheese in dollops all over the dough, spreading it evenly. Arrange half of the roasted tomatoes on top, followed by half of the asparagus mixture.

5. Transfer the pizza to the hot pizza stone or oven rack, and bake until the crust is golden and the cheese has melted, 5 to 7 minutes on the pizza stone or 7 to 10 minutes on the baking sheet.

6. Remove the pizza from the oven and transfer it to a cutting board. Let it rest for 5 minutes. Slice and serve.

7. Repeat from step 3 with the remaining dough ball and toppings.

Mushroom, Oven-Roasted Fennel & Taleggio Pizza

MAKES 2 (12- TO 14-INCH) PIZZAS OR 4 PERSONAL PIZZAS

PREP TIME: 10 minutes
COOK TIME: 1 hour, 25 minutes
TOTAL TIME: 1 hour, 40 minutes
Ingredients:

For the oven-roasted fennel
- 5 fennel bulbs, stems and fronds removed, bulbs cut into ¼-inch-thick slices
- 3 tablespoons extra-virgin olive oil
- ¼ cup grated Parmesan cheese

For the mushrooms and pizza
- Cornmeal or flour, for dusting
- 2 tablespoons extra-virgin olive oil, plus more for brushing
- 4 ounces cremini mushrooms, stems discarded, sliced
- ½ teaspoon dried thyme
- Simply Amazing Pizza Dough or Pro Dough
- ½ pound Taleggio cheese, sliced

Direction:

To make the oven-roasted fennel

1. Preheat the oven to 375°F. Spread the fennel on a baking sheet, toss with the olive oil to coat, then toss with the Parmesan. Bake for 45 minutes, until the fennel is tender.

To make the mushrooms and pizza

1. Preheat the oven and pizza stone (if using) to 500°F. Dust a pizza peel with cornmeal (if using a pizza stone), or brush two baking sheets with olive oil.

2. In a large skillet over medium-high heat, heat the olive oil. When it shimmers, add the mushrooms and thyme. Cook, undisturbed, for 3 to 4 minutes. Give the pan a shake and continue cooking until the mushrooms have released their moisture and are tender, 4 to 5 minutes more.

3. Roll out one of the dough balls to the desired size, and place it on the pizza peel (if using a pizza stone) or on the prepared baking sheet. Prick the dough several times with a fork, then transfer it to the hot stone or oven rack and bake for 3 to 4 minutes, until it just begins to turn color.

4. Remove the crust from the oven and top it with half of the mushrooms and fennel, followed by half of the Taleggio cheese.

5. Transfer the pizza to the hot pizza stone or oven rack, and bake until the crust is golden and the cheese is bubbling, 5 to 7 minutes on the pizza stone or 7 to 10 minutes on the baking sheet.

6. Remove the pizza from the oven and transfer it to a cutting board. Let it rest for 5 minutes. Slice and serve.

7. Repeat from step 3 with the remaining dough ball and toppings.

Butternut Squash Pizza with Bacon & Blue Cheese
MAKES 2 (12- TO 14-INCH) PIZZAS OR 4 PERSONAL PIZZAS

PREP TIME: 10 minutes
COOK TIME: 1 hour
TOTAL TIME: 1 hour, 15 minutes
Ingredients:

- 1 small (1-pound) butternut squash, peeled, seeded, and cut into small dice
- 3 tablespoons extra-virgin olive oil, plus more for brushing
- ¼ teaspoon salt, plus more for finishing
- ⅛ teaspoon freshly ground black pepper, plus more for finishing
- 3 fresh thyme sprigs, stemmed
- 4 slices center-cut bacon
- Cornmeal or flour, for dusting
- Simply Amazing Pizza Dough
- ½ cup grated fontina cheese
- ¼ cup crumbled blue cheese
- 4 cups arugula

Direction:

1. Preheat the oven and pizza stone to 400°F.

2. Spread the butternut squash on a foil-lined baking sheet and drizzle with the olive oil. Season with the salt, pepper, and thyme, and toss well. Bake until the squash is fork tender and golden, about 35 minutes, stirring and rotating the pan halfway through. Remove from the oven and cool briefly.

3. 3 Meanwhile, in a sauté pan over medium heat, brown the bacon until crisp, 2 to 3 minutes per side. Transfer to a paper towel–lined plate and, when cool, roughly chop.

4. 4 Raise the oven temperature to 500°F. Dust a pizza peel with cornmeal (if using a pizza stone), or

brush two baking sheets with olive oil.

5. Roll out one of the dough balls to the desired size, and place it on the pizza peel or on the prepared baking sheet.

6. Spread half of the fontina and blue cheeses evenly over the dough. Top with half of the roasted butternut squash and half of the bacon.

7. Transfer the pizza to the hot pizza stone or oven rack, and bake until the crust is golden and the cheese is bubbly, 5 to 7 minutes on the pizza stone or 7 to 10 minutes on the baking sheet.

8. Remove the pizza from the oven and transfer it to a cutting board. Let it rest for 5 minutes, then top with half of the arugula. Slice and serve.

9. Repeat from step 5 with the remaining dough ball and toppings.

Classic Calzone

MAKES 2 CALZONES

PREP TIME: 10 minutes
COOK TIME: 18 minutes
TOTAL TIME: 30 minutes
Ingredients:

- Extra-virgin olive oil, for greasing and brushing
- ¾ cup fresh ricotta cheese
- ¼ cup grated Parmesan cheese
- ¼ cup grated mozzarella cheese
- 2 tablespoons chopped fresh basil
- ¼ teaspoon salt
- ⅛ teaspoon pepper
- All-purpose flour, for dusting
- ½ recipe (1 ball) Simply Amazing Pizza Dough or Pro Dough divided in half
- ½ cup New York–Style Pizza Sauce

Direction:

1. Preheat the oven to 500°F. Coat a baking sheet lightly with olive oil.

2. In a medium mixing bowl, combine the ricotta, Parmesan, and mozzarella cheeses, chopped basil, salt, and pepper.

3. On a lightly floured work surface, roll out the dough into 2 (6- to 8-inch) circles.

4. Spoon the sauce over each dough circle, leaving a half-inch border.

5. Spread half of the cheese mixture over half of each dough circle.

6. Moisten the edges with water, fold the dough over the filling, and pinch closed from end to end. Brush with olive oil and transfer to the prepared baking sheet.

7. Bake until the crust is golden and firm, 15 to 18 minutes, and serve.

Herbed Goat Cheese & Coppa Calzone

MAKES 2 CALZONES

PREP TIME: 10 minutes
COOK TIME: 18 minutes
TOTAL TIME: 30 minutes

Ingredients:

- Extra-virgin olive oil, for greasing and brushing
- 4 slices sweet coppa, cut into thin strips
- ¾ cup fresh goat cheese, crumbled
- 6 ounces fresh mozzarella cheese, shredded
- 2 tablespoons finely chopped fresh chives
- 2 cups loosely packed chopped fresh flat-leaf parsley
- 2 tablespoons finely chopped fresh oregano
- 2 garlic cloves, minced
- All-purpose flour, for dusting
- ½ recipe (1 ball) Simply Amazing Pizza Dough or Pro Dough ,divided in half

Direction:

1. Preheat the oven to 500°F. Coat a baking sheet lightly with olive oil.

2. In a medium bowl, mix the coppa, goat cheese, mozzarella, chives, parsley, oregano, and garlic with a fork until well combined (add a drop or two of olive oil to soften the mixing process).

3. On a lightly floured work surface, roll out the dough into 2 (6- to 8-inch) circles.

4. Spoon the filling onto half of each circle, leaving a half-inch border. Moisten the edges with water, fold the dough over the filling, and pinch closed from end to end. Brush with olive oil and transfer to the prepared baking sheet.

5. Bake until the crust is golden brown and firm, about 15 to 18 minutes, and serve.

Broccoli Rabe, Sausage & Ricotta Calzone

MAKES 2 CALZONES

PREP TIME: 10 minutes
COOK TIME: 30 minutes
TOTAL TIME: 40 minutes

Ingredients:

- 2 tablespoons extra-virgin olive oil, plus more for greasing and brushing
- 1 bunch broccoli rabe, stems trimmed, rinsed
- 2 garlic cloves, minced
- ¼ teaspoon red pepper flakes
- 3 sweet Italian sausages, removed from casings, sliced
- All-purpose flour, for dusting
- ½ recipe (1 ball) Simply Amazing Pizza Dough or Pro Dough , divided in half
- 1 cup fresh ricotta cheese
- ¼ cup grated mozzarella cheese
- ¼ cup grated Parmesan cheese
- ½ teaspoon salt
- ⅛ teaspoon freshly ground black pepper

Direction:

1. Preheat the oven to 500°F. Coat a baking sheet lightly with olive oil.

2. Bring a large pot of salted water to a boil. Add the broccoli rabe, and blanch for 2 minutes. Using tongs, transfer the broccoli rabe to a large bowl of ice water. Drain, dry, and roughly chop.

3. In a medium sauté pan over medium heat, heat the olive oil. Add the chopped broccoli rabe, and quick sauté for 2 to 3 minutes to finish the cooking process. Add the garlic and red pepper flakes, cook 1 minute more, and transfer to a medium bowl.

4. Add the sausage meat to the pan and cook, stirring frequently with a fork, until no pink color remains, 5 to 6 minutes. Use a slotted spoon to transfer the meat to a bowl.

5. On a lightly floured work surface, roll out the dough into 2 (6- to 8-inch) circles.

6. Spoon the ricotta onto half of each circle, leaving a half-inch border. Top each with half of the mozzarella, Parmesan, salt, and pepper, then the sausage and broccoli rabe.

7. Moisten the edges with water, fold the dough over the filling, and pinch closed from end to end. Brush with olive oil and transfer to the prepared baking sheet.

8. Bake until the crust is golden brown and firm, about 15 to 17 minutes, and serve.

Chicken Pesto Calzone

MAKES 2 CALZONES

PREP TIME: 15 minutes
COOK TIME: 40 minutes
TOTAL TIME: 55 minutes

Ingredients:

For the chicken

- 2 teaspoons extra-virgin olive oil, plus more for greasing

- 1 boneless, skinless chicken breast, pounded between two sheets of wax paper to a uniform thickness
- ½ teaspoon salt
- ⅛ teaspoon freshly ground black pepper

For the calzone
Extra-virgin olive oil, for greasing
All-purpose flour, for dusting
½ recipe (1 ball) Simply Amazing Pizza Dough or Pro Dough ,divided in half
2 slices prosciutto
1 cup fresh ricotta cheese
¼ cup grated mozzarella cheese
½ cup Basil Pesto
⅛ teaspoon freshly ground black pepper
Direction:

To make the chicken

1. Preheat the oven to 350°F. Line the bottom of a baking dish with parchment paper, and rub it and the sides of the dish with a little olive oil.

2. Season the chicken breast with the olive oil, salt, and pepper. Place the chicken breast in the baking dish, pressing it onto the oiled side of the parchment paper, and bake for 20 minutes.

3. Remove the chicken from the oven, let it cool slightly, then cut it against the grain into ½-inch slices.

To make the calzones

1. Increase the oven temperature to 500°F. Lightly grease a baking sheet with oil.

2. On a lightly floured work surface, roll out the dough into 2 (6- to 8-inch) circles.

3. Lay a prosciutto slice on one half of each of the circles, leaving a half-inch border. Top each with half of the chicken, ricotta, mozzarella, and Basil Pesto. Finish with pepper.

4. Moisten the edges with water, fold the dough over the filling, and pinch closed from end to end. Brush with olive oil and transfer to the prepared baking sheet.

5. Bake until the crust is golden brown and firm, about 15 to 18 minutes, and serve.

Bacon, Egg & Sun-Dried Tomato Pesto Calzone
MAKES 2 CALZONES

PREP TIME: 10 minutes, plus 15 minutes to soak
COOK TIME: 25 minutes
TOTAL TIME: 50 minutes
Ingredients:

For the sun-dried tomato pesto
- 4 ounces sun-dried tomatoes, coarsely chopped
- 1½ cups extra-virgin olive oil

For the calzone
- Extra-virgin olive oil, for greasing
- 6 eggs
- ¼ teaspoon salt
- ⅛ teaspoon freshly ground black pepper
- ½ recipe (1 ball) Simply Amazing Pizza Dough or Pro Dough ,divided in half
- 2 ounces pancetta, diced, or center-cut bacon
- ½ cup grated Cheddar cheese
- 1 teaspoon chopped fresh oregano leaves

Direction:

To make the sun-dried tomato pesto

1. In a medium bowl, soak the sun-dried tomatoes in the olive oil for 15 minutes. Transfer the mixture to a blender or food processor and purée to a smooth paste. The pesto can be stored, covered, in the refrigerator for up to 1 week. Stir before using.

To make the calzones

1. Preheat the oven to 500°F. Lightly grease a baking sheet with olive oil.

2. In a medium bowl, whisk the eggs with the salt and pepper.

3. In a medium sauté pan over medium heat, cook the pancetta until brown and crisp, about 6 minutes. Transfer to a paper towel–lined plate to cool, and discard the rendered fat.

4. Melt the butter in the pan. When it foams, add the whisked eggs. Softly scramble the eggs, moving them in the pan until they are no longer liquid, about 2 minutes. Turn off the heat.

5. On a lightly floured surface, roll out the dough into 2 (6- to 8-inch) circles.

6. Spoon a tablespoon of sun-dried tomato pesto on to each dough circle, and spread into a thin, even layer, leaving a half-inch border.

7. Top half of each dough circle with half of the scrambled eggs, pancetta, Cheddar, and oregano.

8. Moisten the edges with water, fold the dough over the filling, and pinch closed from end to end. Brush with olive oil and transfer to the prepared baking sheet.

9. Bake until the crust is golden brown and firm, 15 to 18 minutes, and serve.

Caponata & Goat Cheese Calzone

MAKES 2 CALZONES

PREP TIME: 15 minutes
COOK TIME: 1 hour, 10 minutes
TOTAL TIME: 1 hour 30 minutes
Ingredients:

For the caponata
- 3 eggplants, about 10 inches each, peeled and cut into ½-inch dice
- 20 caper berries, stems removed, sliced thin
- ¼ teaspoon salt
- ⅛ teaspoon freshly ground black pepper
- ¼ teaspoon red pepper flakes
- ¼ cup extra-virgin olive oil
- ¼ cup balsamic vinegar
- 2 tablespoons honey
- 2 medium tomatoes, cored and diced
- ¼ cup pine nuts

For the calzone
All-purpose flour, for dusting
½ recipe (1 ball) Simply Amazing Pizza Dough or Pro Dough , divided in half
¾ cup fresh ricotta cheese
1 cup caponata
¼ cup fresh goat cheese, crumbled
1 tablespoon chopped fresh parsley
Extra-virgin olive oil, for brushing
Direction:

To make the caponata

1. Preheat the oven to 425°F. Line a baking sheet with foil.

2. Spread the eggplant and caper berries on the prepared baking sheet. Season with the salt, black pepper, and red pepper flakes.

3. In a small bowl, whisk together the olive oil, vinegar, and honey. Pour over the eggplant mixture and roast for 40 minutes, tossing the mixture every 10 minutes or so.

4. Add the tomatoes and roast for 10 minutes more. Toss with the pine nuts and cool to room temperature.

To make the calzones

1. Preheat the oven to 500°F.

2. On a lightly floured surface, roll out the dough into 2 (6- to 8-inch) circles.

3. Spoon the ricotta over half of each circle, leaving a half-inch boarder. Top each with half of the caponata, goat cheese, and parsley.

4. Moisten the edges with water, fold the dough over the filling, and pinch closed from end to end. Brush with olive oil and transfer to a lightly oiled baking sheet.

5. Bake until the crust is golden brown and firm, 15 to 18 minutes, and serve.

Slow-Roasted Vegetable Whole-Wheat Calzone

MAKES 2 CALZONES

PREP TIME: 15 minutes
COOK TIME: 55 minutes
TOTAL TIME: 1 hour, 10 minutes
Ingredients:

- 3 tablespoons extra-virgin olive oil, plus more for greasing and brushing
- 2 cups diced butternut squash
- 1 red pepper, diced
- 1 yellow pepper, diced
- 1 cup diced carrots
- 1 teaspoon salt
- ½ teaspoon freshly ground black pepper
- ½ teaspoon dried oregano
- All-purpose flour, for dusting
- ½ recipe (1 ball) Whole-Wheat Pizza Dough , divided in half
- 1 cup New York–Style Pizza Sauce
- ½ cup shredded vegan mozzarella cheese

Direction:

1. Preheat the oven to 450°F. Lightly grease a baking sheet with olive oil.

2. Spread the squash, red pepper, yellow pepper, and carrots on a separate baking sheet, drizzle with the olive oil, toss, and season with the salt, pepper, and oregano. Cook until the vegetables are fork tender and golden in color, about 35 minutes, turning them halfway through. Remove from the oven and cool briefly.

3. On a lightly floured surface, roll out the dough into 2 (6- to 8-inch) circles.

4. Spoon the sauce over the dough, spreading it thinly and evenly, leaving a half-inch border.

5. Top half of each circle with half of the roasted vegetables and vegan cheese.

6. Moisten the edges with water, fold the dough over the filling, and pinch closed from end to end. Brush with olive oil and transfer to the prepared baking sheet.

7. Bake until the crust is golden brown and firm, 15 to 18 minutes, and serve.

Kale, Chard & Caper Whole-Wheat Calzone

MAKES 2 CALZONES

PREP TIME: 15 minutes
COOK TIME: 35 minutes
TOTAL TIME: 50 minutes

Ingredients:

- 2 tablespoons extra-virgin olive oil, plus more for greasing and brushing
- ¼ cup walnuts
- 2 cups roughly chopped kale
- 2 cups roughly chopped Swiss chard
- 2 garlic cloves, minced
- ½ teaspoon red pepper flakes
- 1 tablespoon drained capers
- ½ cup Kalamata or Niçoise olives, pitted and roughly chopped
- 1 teaspoon balsamic vinegar
- ½ cup grated mozzarella cheese
- ½ cup ricotta cheese
- All-purpose flour, for dusting
- ½ recipe (1 ball) Whole-Wheat Pizza Dough , divided in half

Direction:

1. Preheat the oven to 450°F. Lightly grease a baking sheet with olive oil.

2. In a medium sauté pan over medium-low heat, toast the walnuts. Shake the pan frequently and heat the nuts until they are aromatic, about 3 minutes. Roughly chop and set aside.

3. In the same sauté pan over medium heat, heat the olive oil. When it shimmers, add the kale and chard. Cook for 5 minutes, tossing frequently with tongs. Add the garlic and red pepper flakes, and cook for 1 minute more.

4. Transfer the greens to a large sieve and press the liquid from them with the back of a spoon.

5. In a mixing bowl, combine the sautéed greens, capers, olives, and balsamic vinegar. Fold in the mozzarella and ricotta cheeses.

6. On a lightly floured surface, roll out the pizza dough into 2 (6- to 8-inch) circles.

7. Spoon the filling onto half of each circle, leaving a half-inch border. Brush the edges of the dough lightly with water, and fold over. Pinch the dough closed from end to end. Brush with olive oil and transfer to the prepared baking sheet.

8. Bake the calzone until golden brown and bubbly, 20 to 25 minutes, and serve.

Whipped Ricotta, Spinach & Sun-Dried Tomato Calzone

MAKES 2 CALZONES

PREP TIME: 10 minutes, plus 10 minutes to soak
COOK TIME: 30 minutes
TOTAL TIME: 50 minutes

Ingredients:

- 5 tablespoons extra-virgin olive oil, divided, plus more for greasing and brushing
- 3 sun-dried tomatoes
- ⅔ cup ricotta cheese
- ⅓ cup feta cheese
- 2 tablespoons grated Parmesan cheese
- 1 egg yolk
- Salt
- Freshly ground black pepper
- 1 small yellow onion, finely diced (½ cup)
- 2 garlic cloves, minced
- 4 cups baby spinach, stems removed
- All-purpose flour, for dusting
- ½ recipe (1 ball) Simply Amazing Pizza Dough or Pro Dough , divided in half

Direction:

1. Preheat the oven to 500°F. Lightly grease a baking sheet with olive oil.

2. In a small bowl, soak the sun-dried tomatoes in 3 tablespoons of olive oil for 10 minutes. Drain and chop.

3. In a large bowl, mix the ricotta, feta, Parmesan, and egg yolk until well combined. Season with salt and pepper. Set aside.

4. In a sauté pan over medium-high heat, heat the remaining 2 tablespoons of olive oil. When it shimmers, add the onion. Season with salt and pepper and cook, stirring frequently, until the onions are translucent, about 4 minutes. Add the garlic and cook until fragrant, about 1 minute more. Add the spinach to the pan and cook until the leaves have decreased in volume, about 3 minutes.

5. Transfer the spinach mixture to a sieve and, using the back of a spoon, press the moisture from the leaves. Transfer to a cutting board and roughly chop. Fold the chopped spinach and diced sun-dried tomatoes into the ricotta mixture.

6. On a lightly floured surface, roll out the pizza dough into 2 (6- to 8-inch) circles.

7. Spoon the spinach mixture onto half of each circle, leaving a half-inch border. Brush the edges with water and fold the dough over, pinching it closed from end to end. Transfer to the prepared baking sheet and brush lightly with olive oil.

8. Bake until the crust is firm and golden brown, 18 to 20 minutes, and serve.

Soppressata & Pepperoncini Calzone

MAKES 2 CALZONES

PREP TIME: 10 minutes
COOK TIME: 20 minutes
TOTAL TIME: 30 minutes
Ingredients:

- Extra-virgin olive oil, for greasing and brushing
- All-purpose flour, for dusting
- ½ recipe (1 ball) Simply Amazing Pizza Dough or Pro Dough , divided in half
- ½ cup Classic Pizza Sauce
- 6 fresh basil leaves, torn
- ½ teaspoon dried oregano
- 1 garlic clove, minced
- 4 ounces fresh mozzarella cheese
- 3 slices soppressata, sliced into matchsticks
- ¾ cup ricotta cheese
- 1 pepperoncini, roughly chopped

Direction:

1. Preheat the oven to 500°F. Lightly grease a baking sheet with olive oil.

2. On a lightly floured surface, roll out the pizza dough into 2 (6- to 8-inch) circles.

3. Spread the sauce over each dough circle in a thin, even layer, leaving a half-inch border. Top the sauce on each calzone with half of the basil leaves, oregano, and garlic, followed by half of the mozzarella and soppressata pieces on each. Spoon the ricotta over the other ingredients. Top each with a few pieces of chopped pepperoncini.

4. Brush the edges with water and fold the dough over, pinching it closed from end to end. Transfer to the prepared baking sheet and brush lightly with olive oil.

5. Bake in the oven for 18 to 20 minutes, until the dough is golden brown and firm, and serve.

Mushroom & Onion Fold-Over

MAKES 2 CALZONES

PREP TIME: 10 minutes
COOK TIME: 20 minutes
TOTAL TIME: 30 minutes
Ingredients:

- 2 tablespoons extra-virgin olive oil, plus more for greasing and brushing
- 8 ounces button mushrooms, sliced and sautéed
- ½ cup Sweet Onion Jam
- ½ teaspoon dried thyme
- ¼ teaspoon salt
- ⅛ freshly ground black pepper, plus more for finishing
- All-purpose flour, for dusting
- ½ recipe (1 ball) Simply Amazing Pizza Dough , divided in half
- ½ cup grated Gruyère cheese
- ½ cup grated Swiss cheese

Direction:

1. Preheat the oven to 500°F. Lightly grease a baking sheet with olive oil.

2. In a medium bowl, mix the sautéed mushrooms with the Sweet Onion Jam, thyme, salt, and pepper, stirring to combine.

3. On a lightly floured surface, roll out the pizza dough into 2 (6- to 8-inch) circles. Using half each of the grated Gruyère and Swiss cheeses, top each of the circles with a sprinkling, leaving a half-inch border, followed by the mushroom mixture. Top with the remaining Gruyère and Swiss cheeses, and season with pepper.

4. Brush the edges with water and fold the dough over, pinching it closed from end to end. Transfer to the prepared baking sheet, and brush lightly with olive oil.

5. Cook for 18 to 20 minutes, until the cheese has melted and the pizza dough is golden brown, and serve.

Home-Grown Garden Salad

SERVES 4

PREP TIME: 15 minutes
COOK TIME: None
TOTAL TIME: 15 minutes

Ingredients:

- 1 garlic clove, minced
- 3 tablespoons extra-virgin olive oil
- 2 teaspoons freshly squeezed lemon juice
- 2 teaspoons lemon zest
- ½ teaspoon dried oregano
- 3 cups mixed field greens
- 1 red pepper, cut into strips
- 1 yellow pepper, cut into strips
- ½ bunch radishes, sliced thin

- 1 zucchini, ends trimmed, cut lengthwise into thin ribbons
- ¼ teaspoon salt
- ⅛ teaspoon freshly ground black pepper
- ¼ pound Cacio de Roma cheese

Direction:

1. In a salad bowl, whisk the garlic, olive oil, lemon juice, lemon zest, and oregano together.

2. Add the greens, red and yellow peppers, radishes, and zucchini ribbons. Season with the salt and pepper. Toss well, and serve the salad in small bowls topped with Cacio de Roma.

Oven-Roasted Beets with Spinach

SERVES 4

PREP TIME: 15 minutes
COOK TIME: 40 minutes
TOTAL TIME: 50 minutes

Ingredients:

- 4 beets, washed, ends trimmed
- 2 tablespoons extra-virgin olive oil, plus more for rubbing
- 1 tablespoon freshly squeezed orange juice
- 1 tablespoon orange zest
- 1 teaspoon honey
- 2 teaspoons balsamic vinegar
- 3 cups baby spinach or mixed salad greens
- ¼ teaspoon salt
- ⅛ freshly ground black pepper
- 1 (4-ounce piece) pecorino romano cheese

Direction:

1. Preheat the oven to 450°F.

2. Place the beets on squares of aluminum foil, rub with olive oil, and wrap in the foil. Transfer to a baking sheet and cook until easily pierced with the tip of a knife, about 40 minutes. Let cool completely, then rub the skins off the beets (wearing gloves to avoid staining, if preferred). Cut the beets into a medium dice.

3. In a salad bowl, whisk together the orange juice, orange zest, honey, balsamic, and olive oil. Add the diced beets.

4. Just before serving, add the spinach, salt, and pepper, and toss well. Use a vegetable peeler to shave curls of pecorino romano over each serving.

Fennel, Blood Orange, Black Olive & Shrimp Salad

SERVES 4

PREP TIME: 20 minutes
COOK TIME: 10 minutes
TOTAL TIME: 30 minutes
Ingredients:

- 4 blood oranges
- ½ cup, plus 3 tablespoons extra-virgin olive oil
- 1 pound raw shrimp (about 20)
- Salt
- Freshly ground black pepper
- 2 fennel bulbs, outer layer removed, sliced thin
- 4 cups arugula, washed and spun dry
- ½ cup roughly chopped black olives

Direction:

1. Using a large chef's knife, slice the top and bottom of the oranges off so that they stand flat on a cutting board. Slice the peel away from top to bottom in wide strips. When all of the peel has been removed, slice the segments away from the membrane, catching the juice in a small bowl. Set aside.

2. In a large sauté pan over medium-high heat, heat 3 tablespoons of olive oil. Season the shrimp with salt and pepper. When the oil shimmers, add the shrimp to the pan in 2 batches. Cook for 2 minutes per side, until opaque. Transfer to a plate. When cool enough to handle, peel the shrimp, split the backs with a paring knife, and devein.

3. In a salad bowl, use your hands to combine the sliced fennel and arugula. Season with salt and pepper, then add the orange segments and olives.

4. Whisk the remaining ½ cup of olive oil into the bowl of reserved blood orange juice, and dress the salad.

5. Toss the cooked shrimp in the bowl used to mix the olive oil and orange juice, moistening them.

6. Divide the salad among 4 bowls, topping each with a handful of the shrimp. Season with salt and pepper, and serve.

Shaved Brussels Sprout Salad

SERVES 4

PREP TIME: 10 minutes
COOK TIME: 4 minutes
TOTAL TIME: 15 minutes
Ingredients:

- 1 cup hazelnuts or walnuts

- 1½ pounds Brussels sprouts
- ¼ cup extra-virgin olive oil
- Juice of 1 lemon (about 4 tablespoons)
- Sea salt
- Freshly ground black pepper
- 3 tablespoons finely grated pecorino romano cheese

Direction:

1. In a medium sauté pan over medium-low heat, toast the walnuts. Shake the pan frequently and heat the nuts until they are aromatic, about 4 minutes. Remove from the heat and roughly chop. Set aside.

2. Slice each Brussels sprout using a mandoline held over a salad bowl. Hold by the stem end and cut into thin slices. Add the walnuts.

3. In a small bowl, whisk to combine the olive oil and lemon juice. Season with salt and pepper. Dress the salad just before serving, tossing to distribute the dressing. Break the sprout slices into shreds, then sprinkle on the cheese.

The Hampton Classic

SERVES 4 TO 6

PREP TIME: 10 minutes
COOK TIME: 2 minutes
TOTAL TIME: 12 minutes

Ingredients:

- ½ cup shelled pistachios
- 2 tablespoons balsamic vinegar
- 2 tablespoons extra-virgin olive oil
- 3 cups arugula
- 1 cup fresh mint leaves, roughly chopped
- 4 cups diced, seedless watermelon (about 1½-inch dice)
- 1½ cups crumbled feta
- ¼ teaspoon salt
- ¼ teaspoon freshly ground black pepper

Direction:

1. In a small sauté pan over medium heat, swirl the nuts until they are aromatic, about 2 minutes. Remove from the heat and roughly chop.

2. In a small bowl, whisk the vinegar and olive oil together.

3. On a deep platter, use your hands to combine the arugula, mint, and watermelon. Add the feta and pistachios.

4. Drizzle the oil and vinegar over the salad and season with the salt and pepper just before serving.

Jersey Corn & Tomato Salad

SERVES 4

PREP TIME: 15 minutes
COOK TIME: 10 minutes
TOTAL TIME: 25 minutes
Ingredients:

- 1 small red onion, sliced thin
- 8 ears sweet summer corn, shucked
- 3 tablespoons extra-virgin olive oil, plus more for rubbing
- 1 pint multicolored cherry tomatoes
- 1 cup torn fresh basil leaves
- 2 tablespoons chopped fresh oregano
- 2 tablespoons red wine vinegar
- ¼ teaspoon salt, plus extra for the tomatoes
- ⅛ teaspoon freshly ground black pepper

Direction:

1. Preheat the grill or a grill pan on the stove to high heat.

2. In a small bowl of water, soak the onion slices.

3. Rub each ear of corn with a little olive oil. On the grill or grill pan over high heat, cook the corn, about 3 to 4 minutes per side, letting the corn take some char from the grill. Let cool.

4. Meanwhile, strain the onion slices and press between paper towels to dry.

5. In a salad bowl, halve the cherry tomatoes. Lightly salt them to draw a bit of their liquid out.

6. Cut the kernels from the cobs and add to the tomatoes. Toss the salad with the basil leaves and oregano.

7. In a small bowl, whisk to combine the olive oil, vinegar, salt, and pepper. Dress the salad just before serving.

Green Beans with Shallots

SERVES 4

PREP TIME: 10 minutes
COOK TIME: 8 minutes
TOTAL TIME: 18 minutes
Ingredients:

- 1 pound green beans, stem ends trimmed

- 3 tablespoons extra-virgin olive oil
- 2 shallots, peeled and sliced
- Salt
- Freshly ground black pepper
- 3 tablespoons white wine vinegar
- 2 teaspoons Dijon mustard

Direction:

1. Bring a large pot of salted water to a boil. Blanch the beans until just tender, about 4 minutes. Transfer to a bowl of ice water, then drain.

2. In a large sauté pan, heat the olive oil over medium heat. When it shimmers, add the shallots and cook for 4 minutes, until soft and fragrant. Add the green beans and toss to combine. Season with salt and pepper, and transfer to a serving bowl.

3. Add the white wine vinegar and mustard to the still-warm pan, and swirl into the olive oil. Season with salt and pepper, pour over the beans, and serve.

Caesar Salad with Candied Walnuts

SERVES 4

PREP TIME: 15 minutes
COOK TIME: 10 minutes
TOTAL TIME: 25 minutes

Ingredients:

For the dressing
- 4 cloves Balsamic-Roasted Garlic
- 2 teaspoons Dijon mustard
- ½ tablespoon white wine vinegar
- 2 tablespoons sherry vinegar
- 1 egg yolk
- 4 anchovy fillets
- Juice of half a lemon
- ¾ cup extra-virgin olive oil

For the candied walnuts
- 2 egg whites
- 3 tablespoons dark brown sugar
- 2 tablespoons honey
- 2 cups walnut halves

For the salad
1. 2 heads romaine lettuce, ends trimmed, leaves left whole
2. ½ cup grated pecorino romano cheese

3. **Direction:**

To make the dressing

1. In a blender, combine the Balsamic-Roasted Garlic, mustard, white wine and sherry vinegars, egg yolk, anchovies, and lemon juice. With the blender running, add the olive oil in a slow, steady stream until the mixture is smooth. Transfer to a jar, and refrigerate for up to a week.

To make the candied walnuts

1. Preheat the oven to 300°F.

2. In a small bowl, whisk the egg whites until thickened, about 3 minutes. Whisk in the brown sugar and honey. Add the walnuts and stir to coat. Use a slotted spoon to transfer the nuts to a parchment-lined baking tray. Bake for 10 minutes. Let cool completely. The nuts can be stored in an airtight container for up to 2 weeks.

To make the salad

1. In a large salad bowl, toss the dressing, romaine leaves, and cheese. Serve immediately, topping each salad serving with a few candied walnuts.

Kale Salad with Anchovy Vinaigrette

SERVES 4

PREP TIME: 10 minutes
COOK TIME: None
TOTAL TIME: 10 minutes

Ingredients:

- 2 anchovy fillets
- 1 garlic clove, smashed
- 12 fresh basil leaves, roughly chopped
- 2 teaspoons Dijon mustard
- Juice of 1 lemon
- ¾ cup extra-virgin olive oil
- 4 cups ribbed, chopped kale
- ¼ teaspoon salt
- ⅛ teaspoon freshly ground black pepper
- ½ cup grated pecorino romano cheese

Direction:

1. In a blender, pulse to combine the anchovies, garlic, basil leaves, mustard, and lemon juice.

2. With the blender running, add the olive oil in a slow, steady stream.

3. In a salad bowl, dress the kale leaves with the dressing. Rub the dressing into the kale leaves, coating each leaf.

4. Season the salad with the salt and pepper, sprinkle with the cheese, and serve.

Celery & Chickpea Salad

SERVES 4

PREP TIME: 10 minutes
COOK TIME: None
TOTAL TIME: 10 minutes
Ingredients:

- 1 garlic clove, roughly chopped
- 3 tablespoons extra-virgin olive oil
- Juice of 1 lemon
- ⅛ teaspoon ground cumin
- ¼ teaspoon salt
- ⅛ teaspoon freshly ground black pepper
- 5 celery stalks, sliced thin on a mandoline (3 cups)
- 1 (15.5-ounce) can chickpeas, rinsed and drained
- ½ cup flat-leaf parsley leaves, roughly chopped
- Leafy greens from the celery, roughly chopped

Direction:

1. In a salad bowl, crush the garlic with a pestle or meat tenderizer. Add the olive oil, lemon juice, cumin, salt, and pepper, and whisk to combine.

2. Add the celery, chickpeas, parsley, and celery greens. Toss thoroughly, and serve.

9 789858 879603 05